Tambora

Tambora

Travels to Sumbawa and the
mountain that changed the world

Derek Pugh

Cover and Interior Design: Raven Tree Design

National Library of Australia Cataloguing-in-Publication entry :

Pugh, Derek, author.

Title: Tambora : travels to Sumbawa and the mountain that changed the world / Derek Pugh.

ISBN: 9780992355845

Subjects:: Pugh, Derek

Weather--Effect of volcanic eruptions on.

Tambora, Mount (Indonesia)--Eruption, 1815

Sumbawa Island (Indonesia)--Description and travel.

Sumbawa Island (Indonesia)--Social life and customs.

Sumbawa Island (Indonesia)--History.

Dewey Number: 915.9865

Also by Derek Pugh

Turn Left at the Devil Tree, 2013

Tammy Damulkurra, 1995 (2nd edition 2013)

The Owner's Guide to the Teenage Brain, 2011

Contact: *derekpugh1@gmail.com*

Website: *www.derekpugh.com.au*

To Harry and Roy.
Adventure is there for the taking.

Contents

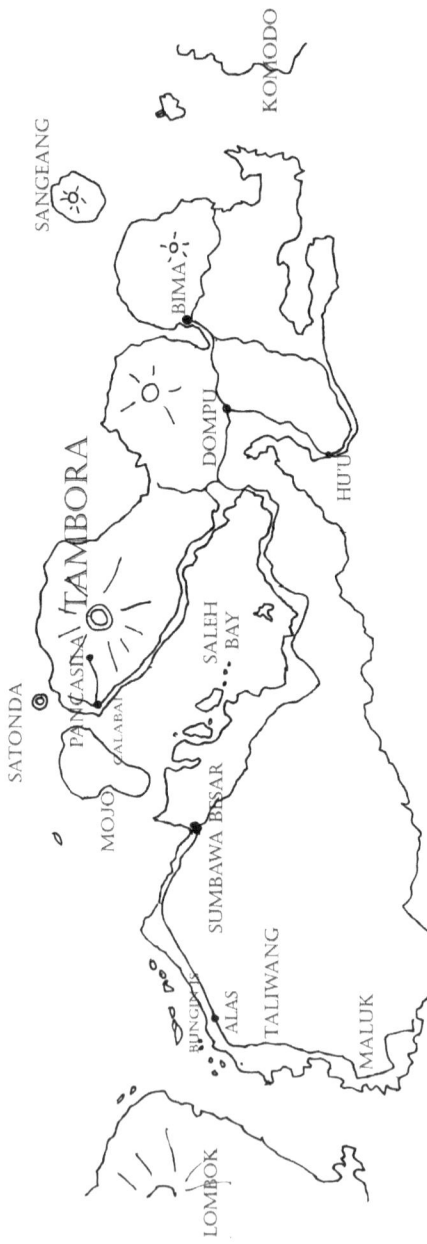

SANGEANG

KOMODO

SATONDA

TAMBORA

PANCASILA

CALABAI

BIMA

DOMPU

SALEH
BAY

HU'U

MOJO

SUMBAWA BESAR

BUNGIN

ALAS

TALIWANG

MALUK

LOMBOK

S U M B A W A

Prologue

It all started two hundred years or so ago on the fifth day of April in 1815. For over five days a huge volcano named *Gunung Tambora* that towered over the remote island of Sumbawa in the East Indies, erupted in a spectacular forty–three kilometre high, multi–column display of fire and smoke.

Indonesia, as the East Indies are now known, takes up a lengthy part of the *Pacific Ring of Fire* where volcanoes line the edges of massive tectonic plates. Hundreds of them stand in sentinel all along the shores of the Pacific Ocean like giant Viking beacons.

Indonesia is a massive country. Thousands of islands stretch for more than 5000 kilometres from West Papua in the east to Aceh on the western tip of Sumatra. There are more than one hundred and twenty volcanoes in Indonesia alone, and many are intermittently active. Somewhere in the archipelago, you can expect at least one of them to be rumbling, or even erupting, at any one time.

Most of their conniptions are small, but they still cause local disruption and a little damage. Tambora's awakening was very different indeed. The April 1815 eruption was probably the biggest eruption the earth has seen in 10,000 years. Its ash cloud spread over an area the size of Australia, blocking out the sun in many parts for several days. People waited, terrified perhaps, as they scurried from shelter to shelter in pitch black at noon in search of sustenance, friends or family. As the ash fell to earth it buried crops, collapsed roofs, and sank ships. Tens of thousands of people perished immediately—plucked from their homes and hurled skywards by the pyroclastic winds or crushed and cooked by superheated pyroclastic flows, swept away by tsunamis, bombarded by huge lava bombs, or in the months and years after the eruption, they died a slower, equally tragic death, through disease or starvation.

But that wasn't all. Tambora pumped millions of tons of chemicals into the stratosphere and formed an aerosol blanket of sulphuric acid that covered our planet and lingered for at least three years, reflecting much of the sun's heat and light back into space. The result was a cooler earth and the *Year Without Summer*. In post–war Europe, North America, and Asia crops failed, diseases like cholera took hold, and civil unrest grew. Millions of people had died or had been displaced, and whole populations had changed dramatically.

And here was the genesis of both Frankenstein's monster and the bicycle: the continuous foul weather in Switzerland caused Mary Shelley to stay indoors where, instead of larking about in boats on Lake Geneva and whiling away the long summer evenings reading poetry, she wrote of Dr Frankenstein and his monster, arguably the first science fiction novel the world had ever seen. At the same time in Germany, as horses starved around them because the weather was too inclement to grow hay, two enterprising young men invented the first bicycle. Both were products of Tambora.

As a resident of Sumbawa's neighbouring island of Lombok, I had long been intrigued and drawn to this island, and the mountain that had such a wide and dramatic effect on our planet. So, with the bicentenary of the eruption looming, I took a number of trips by motorcycle through Sumbawa to see what life is like in modern day Indonesia, explore for myself the island, and climb the mountain that had changed the world.

I met tiny, yet experienced race jockeys the same age as my pre–schooler son and an aged princess who is a direct descendent of the Rajah of Bima who was ruling at the time of the eruption; I visited mining towns, surf camps, and the small island of Bungin whose residents claim they live on the most densely populated island in the world and whose goats are rumoured to survive eating nothing but plastic and rags. Everywhere I went Tambora was omnipresent, like a school bully leering over my shoulder. And when, at last, I climbed to its crater rim, stared out across a hole seven kilometres in diameter and a nearly a kilometre deep, and smelled its sulphurous fumes, I was in awe. Tambora is an extreme mountain in every way. Huge gas plumes regularly burst from vents far below where I stood on the precipice, and the continuous crashing of rocks—falling and echoing around the crater's cliffs—gave me a feeling that this mountain is still very much alive and just biding its time.

Then, looking east to Sangeang Api, west to Rinjani on Lombok, and further to Agung on Bali, I realised that any of these huge volcanoes, which stand in line like giant boils along the archipelago, could take their turn and release their fury on our planet, just like Tambora did two hundred years ago. Standing on the summit, I wondered if we would be prepared. Now, writing safely in my home, I still doubt that we would be.

Chapter 1.

A Destination Just Missed

From the deck of the *Antares,* Tambora looked enormous but flat—more like a giant upturned pie than the classic volcano. The mountain was purple in shadow, out of focus through the early morning November haze.

We'd been on the *Antares* for a few days after leaving Teluk Nara, in North West Lombok. Fabien, owner and captain of this small charter yacht, was humming in the galley where daily he would create bread masterpieces that stereotypically tagged him as being a Frenchman and proud of it.

This was my third trip in waters close to Tambora. Several years before I had taken a tourist boat through the Flores Sea from Komodo to Lombok and for two days had cruised past the mountain off its northern coast, stopping twice along the way: firstly at a boat building village and then at the small island and wildlife reserve of Moyo to see the waterfalls. Tambora was calling like a siren as we passed, a destination just missed; a place I wanted to see.

I had had a second near miss, also travelling on the *Antares*, when we passed by on a diving trip to Komodo National Park, and the surly siren of Tambora had again called me to attend her, to no avail.

Then, on this third trip, I had tagged along with Mark Heyward and his sons with our host, Andrew, all friends and neighbours in Lombok. Andrew is an agronomist, who was seeking new areas to grow tobacco and trees, and pairing a yacht with a motorbike seemed the perfect way for him to get into remote parts of Sumbawa. Mark and I had jumped at the chance to travel with him, and at the last minute, he had agreed that Mark could bring his two boys, Rory (11) and Harry (8).

Before breakfast, Rory and I were sitting on the cabin roof watching the sea slide past. The boys had both tried SCUBA diving the day before off Moyo Island and were agog at the new world that had opened up to them. I was trying to get Rory interested in Mount Tambora.

"Two hundred years ago, if you were diving here, you'd have found nearly everything in the sea dead. The land was dead too. Look at Tambora—see how it's flat on top? It used to be shaped like a proper cone—more like Rinjani in Lombok or Agung in Bali but bigger. It was four thousand three hundred metres high, but in 1815, it blew up in what people say was the loudest noise ever heard, and it lost its top. That was nearly 200 years ago. Millions of tons of rock and dust were blown up. Can you imagine what that would have been like?"

"I guess you wouldn't want to be in this boat here when that happened," said Rory.

"You're right. There were tsunamis and enormous floating islands of pumice—you know that rock that floats? Boats weren't much good to you then. It caused what they called the '*Year Without Summer*' in the northern hemisphere—Europe and America froze, and they couldn't grow food, so people starved—and not just for one year as the 'volcanic winter' lasted at least three years. In India and China, the monsoon never arrived, so they had no food there either. There was civil unrest and riots, and thousands of people moved or emigrated as climate refugees. In America they used to call the year 'eighteen hundred and froze to death'. Oh, and Frankenstein's monster was born."

"Really?"

"Well, the author couldn't go outside in Switzerland because it was so cold and wet, so she stayed in and wrote *Frankenstein*."

We talked for a while about how everything on earth was connected and how a volcano in Indonesia could make it rain in Ireland. On the day we'd left Lombok, I had quickly printed a few pages of information about Tambora I had taken from Wikipedia, and I clutched them, reading out bits and pieces of interest as we sailed into the bay, but there wasn't much substance to what I read, and I was starting to have more questions than answers.

We entered the giant shallow bay, which almost cuts Sumbawa in two, named Saleh Bay. *Saleh* in Bahasa Indonesia means anything from pious or religious to godly and virtuous. It's an enormous bay where excellent fishing has sustained populations of fishermen for thousands of years. Tambora loomed darkly over it on its own peninsula in the north called the Sanggar Peninsula. Behind the scent of salt and the sea we could faintly smell smoke coming from a fire on the coast. A white–bellied sea eagle cruised across our view, silhouetted against the mountain. Occasionally flying fish burst from the water before skimming tens of metres away from us on huge gossamer wings before plunging back into the depths. The water was calm, and there was little wind, so Fabien didn't bother to get the crew to raise the sails; we had the engine running most of the day.

As we moved into the southern parts of Saleh Bay, we found the water to be increasingly unpleasant and not at all 'godly'. The water was hot, murky, and thick with giant white jellyfish, like anaemic pulsing Frisbees, and millions of small red jellyfish spread like autumn leaves caught in the wind. Our propeller would mince them up and churn them into a soup behind us. We passed more and more long wooden boats with fishermen, holding poles with scoop nets, and after a while we realised they were catching the giant jellyfish. They would stop their boats and just scoop the large white discs out of the water.

"What for? Why do they want jellyfish? They are disgusting," said Harry.

None of us really knew. "Perhaps they eat them here like in China," I replied. I'd never heard of Indonesians eating jellyfish, but it was clear they were being harvested, and in large numbers too, so someone must be doing something with them. Perhaps they exported them.

We eventually left the brown jellyfish soup behind and gratefully motored into deeper clear water towards a group of small islands to moor for the night. The island Fabien had chosen rose nearly vertically out of a ring of coral and sand. In the water on either side of us were lines of black plastic buoys suspending baby oyster shells, at this stage called spats, in flat wire racks in the current. The oysters spend their days filtering the water and growing big enough to creat the pearls that command such high prices in the showrooms in Lombok and across the world.

In the last daylight, the boys went snorkelling along a small reef a short way from the boat, and the crew threw fishing lines into the deep to try their luck. On the island, steep cliffs striped with the trails of goats wrapped around a small beach and the dark patch of forest behind it and, as darkness fell, a single light marked a pearl man's thatched cottage where he lived to guard the precious oyster shells. He had retreated to his house by the time we arrived, so we never saw him, and his tiny generator sputtered out soon after dark leaving us with the gentle lapping of waves, the occasional slap of a jumping fish, and a zillion stars reflecting on the black waters. Never too far from a guitar, the serenity brought out the music in Mark, and he sang the songs he'd written during a lifetime of knocking around Indonesia and later recorded on an album he named *Crazy Little Heaven* as a tribute to the country he loved.

Against the night sky, Tambora was a distant brooding hulk two thousand eight hundred and fifty metres high. It looked big, but we knew it was a far cry from its previously more majestic height of about forty thousand three hundred metres. From the sea, it appeared old and beaten, not young and fresh like the cinder cones of Mount Agung in Bali or Mount Merapi in Java, which I'd climbed before its eruption in 2010, but I knew that Tambora was also still active and occasionally stirred to remind the locals to beware. The government had warned of a potential eruption only a few months before as the monster's belly had rumbled, but it was quiet now—for the moment.

Andrew's plan was to go ashore and use a motorbike to do his surveys on land, and we would go the other way by car back to Lombok and leave Tambora behind. For a while, I pondered how easy it would be to ask Fabien to drop me on the northern shore of the bay and then leave me to slowly wander up the slopes to sit on the crater's edge and imagine the mighty power of the eruption that was big enough to change the world's climate. There were villages on the lower slopes, and surely, there must be footpaths going up the sides. But with time short, nothing to wear on my feet except rubber thongs, and with zero preparation, I pushed these thoughts aside.

The next day we left the yacht and motored south by inflatable dinghy, across the bay to a small village marked on the map where we'd organised to be met by a car for the drive back to the ferry to Lombok. This was Labuhan Sangoro. We could smell it long before we neared the dock. A strong rotten fish odour grabbed the back of our throats. We could see many of the long thin fishing boats, like those we'd passed at sea, tied along the pebbly beach to the right of the village near a jetty. The water surrounding them was deep with jelly. Large plastic tubs of jellyfish sat on the decks of the boats and on the jetty, and people were taking them out one by one and cutting the bells away from the central core, known as the 'jellyfish head' then casting the bells into the sea.

The stone jetty was slippery with their pink slime and the air so thick with their smell that on this day, they didn't seem the least bit appetising, but when I later looked up jellyfish recipes, I found they appear quite commonly in Japanese and Chinese cuisine, and this was indeed a factory for their export.

We slid as much as walked through the slimy length of the jetty to the beach, where there were rows of large vats full of the heads. The Indonesian workers washed the jellyfish heads before salting them and packing them into drums ready for transporting to China and they were happy for us to visit and take photographs and ask them about what they were doing. Some of them were doing the washing, standing thigh deep in the briny vats of jelly and churning the water with their feet, whilst others were sorting and carrying them to groups of women who quickly salted the washed heads and packed them into white plastic drums. There were hundreds of drums already full, sealed, and ready to go.

A lone, neatly dressed Chinese man was standing quietly in the shade under a tarpaulin holding a clipboard. I said hello, but he knew neither English nor Indonesian and looked stressed when I was speaking to him, so I left him to his work. It was his job to ensure that every salted jellyfish head packed into each drum was high quality and prepared correctly, weigh the drums, and pay the fishermen. The Indonesians he watched bore his presence stoically, but there seemed to be no communication between them, and one or two of them whispered to us about him and rolled their eyes. It all seemed a bit odd, and the poor bloke must have had one of the loneliest jobs, but the jellyfish industry was clearly alive and well, servicing a strong demand from China.

Andrew had organised a car to pick us up at Sangoro, but we were early and needed to wait for a couple of hours for it to arrive. To fill in the time we hired a small boat to take a tour of the water in front of the village, which gave us respite from the all pervading smell at the factory. The boatman had anchored his boat in knee–deep water and wading through hundreds of the cast off jellyfish bells to get to it was unpleasant indeed, as the rotting jelly clung to our skin, but we were able to wash our legs in the clear water as we moved out and headed across to where the villagers moored their boats.

From the boat, Sangoro didn't appear to be a wealthy place, and I thought at first that it might just be a seasonal village used during the jelly–fishing season. The unattractive ramshackle stilted huts and rubbish strewn beaches around the bay had a temporary feel about them, but behind them I could see a modern school building and the short minarets of a small mosque. These and the power lines stretching to the houses told me Sangoro is, in fact, a permanent settlement. We could see large numbers of small children playing among the houses and hear their shouts and laughter. The stringent smell of wood smoke and sweeter odours of someone's cooking reached us as we motored close to the shore, providing a pleasant contrast to the smell at the jetty.

The water was warm and shallow. We could see thousands of *bulu babi*, or 'pig hair' sea urchins, spearing the water with a multitude of twenty centimetre long spines like giant black rambutans scattered across the ground. In these numbers, they are always the mark of a disturbed environment as they move in large clusters feeding on the seabed. The water was so clear that we could see bright iridescent blue spots among their spines.

I wondered if there were other villages like this one collecting jellyfish in Saleh Bay and asked the boatman.

"Yes, there are others, further west," he replied as he motored through several dozen boats moored in front of the village. A few of them were larger than the thin boats we had encountered so far, with rude cabins built precariously on the decks and washing lines tied between short masts. A couple of them were very large with long outrigger supported platforms on either side, and I guessed they had the role of a 'factory ship', but the boatman just shrugged when I asked him. He then said that for most of the year they go fishing for a more traditional catch, and I assumed these larger boats would be used for fishing trips further afield than the local waters. I concluded that an economic choice had been made by the community—jellyfish must pay better than the normal catch, so for a while the fish of Saleh Bay were a little safer. I wondered what the locals were now eating instead.

When our car finally arrived, it took us an hour on a rough dirt track before we reached the highway and turned west towards the port where a ferry would take us to Lombok, three hours drive away on the other side of the region's biggest city, Sumbawa Besar. Tambora was long behind and now no longer visible. I had been near to it three times but had been left wanting, and I discovered it had an inextricably powerful pull on me; I planned to one day come back and climb it to look down into the crater which was so violent two centuries ago. In the meantime, I could do some research and find out more about the effect the eruption had had on the local people and the world's climate.

Chapter 2.

1815

What is now the country of Indonesia, but was then the East Indies, had been through a bit of a tussle between various European states in the early eighteen hundreds. The *commercial* masters of Java in Holland (through the Dutch East indies Company, VOC) had been overrun by the armies of Napoleon Bonaparte, and the English didn't like the idea of the French taking control of Dutch 'colonies' one little bit. So, with puffed out chests of their own importance and a military skirmish that lasted about forty–five days (both against the French and the Dutch management), they took over the East Indies as a 'temporary' protection measure and selflessly safeguarded Holland's interests whilst the Dutch were busy looking after their problems at home.

The man to take the helm was Sir Stamford Raffles. He had been working in Penang for the British East India

Company and through deft political management and sponsorship by members of the aristocracy (specifically Lord Minto who was the man in charge of India). Raffles was appointed as the Lieutenant Governor of Java in 1811. By most accounts, he was a decent man who spoke Malay well and was interested in people, culture, plants, and animals. He was against slavery, the opium trade, torture, and other common inhumane practices of the time. He led a fruitful life as he also had time to be the founding father of Singapore and the Regents Park Zoo in London.

The English rule in Indonesia was brief, a mere five years, and Tambora's eruption just happened to fall under Raffles' watch. The Dutch, who had been in the East Indies for several centuries, recorded little about the culture and physical nature of the archipelago. It seems they were there only to see what they could produce and take and cared little for the locals—the East Indies were business, *not* colony. They were based in Batavia (now known as Jakarta), and although not in effective control of far flung islands like Sumbawa until the late nineteenth century, the Dutch wielded much influence with the sultans of the islands.

Raffles was more of a humanist. British 'residents' were sent to all corners of the archipelago, and one of the things Raffles insisted upon was report making. We know much about what happened in Sumbawa from his memoirs and reports he ordered his officers to gather. Raffles did not ever go to Sumbawa himself.

Before 1815, Mount Tambora was one of the tallest mountains in Indonesia. It must have been a magnificent sight—a huge stratovolcano with a classic double peaked cone proudly reaching into the sky far enough to create its own weather. At over four thousand three hundred metres

high and with a base diameter of sixty kilometers, it dominated Sumbawa and dwarfed Lombok's Mount Rinjani at
three thousand seven hundred and twenty–six metres. It was
a valued landmark for anyone passing on a ship.

After five thousand years of dormancy, the mountain's
belly started rumbling from as early as 1812. In the village
of Tambora, a community of about twelve thousand souls
lived what appears to have been a cultured and well-off life.
Judging by remnant pottery, they had cultural links to the
Philippines and Cambodia, and they are known to have
spoken a language unrelated to Bimanese or Sumbawan. The
sultan, Raja Abdul Gafur, and his people would have had
no idea of the unprecedented cataclysm Tambora's rumbling
was heralding, and life would have pretty much continued
as normal. Even though they were used to the mountain
being quiet, its slow awakening over three years or so meant
that smoke and a little ash had become a common sight, so
perhaps to them there didn't seem too much to worry about.

By 1814, Tambora was upping the ante. John Crawfurd,
an eyewitness, sailed past and wrote an account of a mountain that was already misbehaving badly:

> "... Tomboro was in a state of great activity. At a distance
> the clouds of ashes which it threw out blackened our one side of
> the horizon in such a manner as to convey the appearance of a
> threatening tropical squall (in fact it was mistaken for one and the
> commander... took in sail, and prepared to encounter it). As we
> approached... ashes even fell on the deck."

These days much of the leeward southern and western
lowlands around Tambora are seasonally very dry and the
vegetation boasts little other than stony grasslands and
prickly *Acacia* trees. It is not until you reach the northern
'weather' side or get to some altitude that the forest starts

taking advantage of mountain-generated rainfall. The major agricultural industry for the area is rearing horses, cattle, and buffalo along the coast, as it was before the eruption, but the effect of being on the leeward side of a shorter mountain would, no doubt, have made a difference to local micro–climates, so the area is surely different than it was prior to 1815. A Dutchman named Radermacher described it in 1786:

> "A tiny barren rocky district where nothing grows in the mountains but a little paddy, hardly enough to feed its inhabitants, who therefore obtain this from traders in exchange for the products which are found in abundance in the forests and are available in their purest form here, and by which, as well as by horse breeding, the king, nobles and subjects are compensated annually for the barrenness of their country."

During this time, there were six sultanates in Sumbawa (Sumbawa, Bima, Dompo, Sanggar, Pekat, and Tambora), and villages were spread across the island, often built beside rivers and teak forests. Most villages were located away from the coast a few kilometres or up in the hills as a protection against marauding slave traders and pirates. Even the village of Tambora, a kingdom in its own right, was at least five kilometres from the sea. Much of the island was fertile with good rainfalls, and trade routes had for centuries existed between the sultanates and further afield as far as Vietnam, Cambodia, China, and the rest of South East Asia. Sumbawa was well known for its horses and sappan wood (a medicine and red dye for cloth) and a range of crops such as garlic, corn, and rice.

The sultan and the doomed residents of Tambora had no textbooks of vulcanology to consult; they had no idea that, fifteen hundred metres beneath them, there was a huge chamber of hydrous magma heating and churning like an

Irish stew in a pressure cooker at more than nine hundred degrees Celsius. If people had become complacent, we can imagine their surprise and horror when on the fifth of April the earth shook, and an eruption with 'thunderous detonation sounds' sent ash and rocks far into the atmosphere above them.

In 2004, the volcanologist Haraldur Sigurdsson managed to excavate one of their houses, which he had found it to be completely carbonised from the heat. He also found the remains of two people still inside. Maybe rumbles and small tremors had awakened them over the past few weeks and months but as little damage had occurred they were intent on staying home and getting on with life. The noise of the eruption was so loud people heard it twelve hundred and sixty kilometres away in Batavia (now Jakarta) on Java, and even as far as Ternate on the Molucca Islands, fourteen hundred kilometres away. It must have been as agonising as it was deafening for those who lived on the mountain's slopes, and perhaps it was the last sound they heard.

Only three hundred and fifty kilometres away at Makassar, the commander of the *Benares* wrote:

> "On the fifth of April a firing of cannon was heard at Makassar: the sound appeared to come from the southward, and continued at intervals all the afternoon. Towards sunset the reports seemed to approach much nearer, and sounded like heavy guns occasionally, with slighter reports between."

In East Java, ash began to fall by the sixth of April, and they could hear the eruption continuing right through to the tenth. Sir Stamford Raffles wrote in his memoir:

> "The first explosions were heard on this Island in the evening of 5 April, they were noticed in every quarter, and continued at intervals until the following day. The noise was, in the first instance, almost

universally attributed to distant cannon; so much so, that a detachment of troops were marched from Djocjocarta [Yogyakarta] in the expectation that a neighbouring post was attacked, and along the coast boats were in two instances dispatched in quest of a supposed ship in distress."

The village of Sanggar, which was on the eastern coast of Tambora about thirty kilometres from the crater, requested help from Bima, and the British resident sent a man named Israël there to see what they could do. Not knowing that he had been sent to his death, Israël arrived on the ninth of April. He was never seen again.

At seven o'clock in the evening of the tenth of April Tambora erupted again with even greater explosions. The volcano hurled colossal amounts of magma, dust and gases up to forty three kilometres into the atmosphere. (The material ejected out of volcanoes collectively is called tephra. This includes ash, lapilli (cinders), and volcanic bombs, which are larger rocks). By this time the Sultan of Sanggar, perhaps the possessor of the fastest horses, or the most industrious slaves, had managed to escape to Dompu. There are tales of him and his entourage galloping down ridges with rivers of lava to the left and the right. The sultan survived the eruption but most of the rest of the population of Sanggar, including the unfortunate Israël, died in the violent pyroclastic currents. The sultan was a credible eyewitness, and in August he was able to report to Lieutenant Owen Phillips, sent by Raffles to survey the damage and take aid for the populace, that:

> "...three distinct columns of flame burst forth near the top of Tomboro Mountain... and after ascending separately to a very great height, their tops united in a troubled and confused manner...
>
> "In a short time the whole mountain next to Sang'ir appeared like a body of liquid fire, extending itself in every direction. The fire and columns of flame continued to rage with unabated fury, until

the darkness caused by the quantity of falling matter obscured it at about 8 pm. Stones... fell very thick at Sang'ir; some as large as two fists, but generally not larger than walnuts.

"Between 9 and 10 pm, ashes began to fall, and soon after a violent whirlwind ensued, which blew down nearly every house in the village of Sang'ir, carrying the *ataps* or roof, and light parts away with it. In the parts of Sang'ir adjoining Tomboro its effects were much more violent, tearing up the largest trees and carrying them into the air, together with men, horses, cattle and whatever else came within its influence.

"The whirlwind lasted about an hour. No explosions were heard until the whirlwind ceased, at about 11 am. From midnight till the evening of the 11th they continued without intermission; after that time their violence moderated, and they were only heard at intervals, but the explosions did not cease entirely until the 15th July."

'Whirlwinds' are formed as superheated air rushes upwards, creating a vacuum beneath and surrounding air races in to replace it. They must have been a horror to be caught in, but the scariest and most lethal of all volcanic events to my mind, pyroclastic flows, were soon to race down the mountain to the sea as parts of the ash column above collapsed back to earth. They fell on all sides of the peninsula, and some travelled as far as twenty or thirty kilometres in a matter of minutes. Raja Abdul Gafur and all the residents of the village of Tambora, all the forest and its wildlife, and anyone anywhere near the volcano was wiped away or cooked and buried by the superheated flows.

As the flows met the cold sea water on each side of the mountain, violent explosions of ash and steam occurred as the water was instantly vaporised. This added to the rising ash cloud, so together the column was nearly forty kilometres in diameter. The mountain kept bellowing for a number of hours, and its ash cloud mushroomed in all directions.

Within twenty–four hours, the cloud had spread out to about the size of Australia, blocking out all light beneath it for both the eleventh and twelfth of April. Some witnesses described the dark as being 'darker than the darkest night'.

The eruption and its violent interactions of the sea and the pyroclastic flows sent tsunamis, up to four metres high, in all directions. These walls of water washed away unknown numbers of people in Sumbawa Besar, Lombok, and even Bali, Sulawesi, and Malaysia. In some of these places, the cloud was so dense it remained dark for several more days and in Batavia there were claims they could even smell the eruption.

In Bima, it remained dark until noon on the twelfth of April. Most of the houses had had such a build–up of ash on their roofs that they collapsed, including the home of the British resident whose description of the sound of the eruption—like a 'heavy mortar' fired close to his ear—gives an idea of its loudness. Bima is sixty five kilometres from Tambora.

The eruption was by far the deadliest in recorded history, and only the death toll of the 2004 tsunami disaster surpasses it in number of people killed. Scientists estimate that Tambora hurled between a hundred and a hundred and fifty cubic kilometres of tephra into the atmosphere. The death toll rose from twelve thousand people in the first few minutes to ninety two thousand in the weeks following to an estimated total of one hundred and twenty five thousand over the next few months. The mountain lost more than fourteen hundred metres in height and left a caldera that is seven kilometres in diameter and eight hundred metres deep.

Scientists award the eruption a VEI 7. The VEI, or the Volcanic Explosivity Index, is understood most easily in comparison to the more familiar Richter scale for earthquakes; each number is ten times the previous number, so an earthquake of six on the Richter scale is ten times bigger than an earthquake of five. Earthquakes of five or six are everyday occurrences somewhere in the Pacific "Ring of Fire"—you get a bit of a shake for a second or two and then things quieten down. In 2004, the earthquake that hit Sumatra and caused the tsunami which killed two hundred thousand people was a niner! Nine on the Richter scale is 10x10x10x10 or ten thousand times an earthquake of the more familiar five. With a whole lot of shaking like that, it is impossible to walk, and buildings collapse like cards, a lot of people die, and share markets tumble.

The Volcanic Explosivity Index works like that too within a range of zero to eight. Each level is a logarithmic progression ten times the previous. Tambora at a VEI of seven is thus ten times the more famous Mount Krakatau that rates a six, and a million times more explosive than the lava oozing volcanoes of Hawaii which rate zero or one. The index is a measure of how much stuff is ejected and the height of the cloud that is produced, so small explosions rate a two and most volcanoes rarely rise above a four or five.

In the United States, Mount St Helens erupted in 1980 with a huge ash cloud and incredible force, and it was VEI 5. It is called "very large", though this is a little misleading because it exploded sideways rather than straight up, so its height was low. Mount St Helens was on the nightly news for weeks, and some of the most famous footage of volcanic carnage comes from it. Mount Vesuvius, during the famous eruption in AD79 that wiped out Pompeii and other Roman towns was ten times that, rating a VEI 6, like Krakatau in 1883. These mountains are famous because their eruptions were *huge,* and they star in Hollywood films and in school science books.

Tambora by comparison is little known. Volcanologists have a range of adjectives to suit eruptions on a parallel scale to the numeric VEI: Moderate, Large, Very Large (like Mt. St Helens), and Huge (like Vesuvius, Pinatoba and Krakatau). But these are run of the mill. Tambora's eruption in 1815 was *colossal,* and a hundred times the size of Mount St Helens! And even that isn't the highest level. That gets awarded to a mountain that erupted about seventy four thousand years ago in Sumatra named Mount Toba. These days Toba has a crater lake a hundred kilometres long that was created by an eruption so large that the boffins reserve a word for it that I have only ever heard children use before— the eruption of Mount Toba in Sumatra scored a VEI 8 and is described as *humungous*. It was a thousand times the size of Mount St. Helens and ten times Mount Tambora. Toba was so large that the 'volcanic winter' it created would have lasted for many years and many species around the planet must have been annihilated or driven close to extinction. This may have nearly included our own species—it is thought that ninety percent of all humans may have died during this time. *Humungous* is the term for the biggest so far, and if ever there is an eruption off the scale with a VEI 9, we will have to invent a new word to describe it, just before our planet is torn apart. Quote me if you need to, I suggest a new word: *supermungous.*

Another colossal eruption thought to also have a VEI 7, but is even less well known, was a mountain from Lombok, which erupted in the thirteenth century, only two hundred kilometres or so from Tambora. This mountain, known as Samalas, is essentially the same volcano, though with a different peak, known as Rinjani. Until very recently it was called by scientists the "Great 1258 Unknown" as no one knew where it was. Some scientists now say its eruption was the cause of the 'little ice–age' when medieval chroniclers in Europe told of freezing summers and warm winters and of floods and failed harvests. Indonesian records written on palm leaves from Java describe a massive and deadly eruption, which wiped out a city called Pamatan on Lombok. No one today knows where Pamatan stood or if it will be possible to dig it up one day like Pompeii, and there's still much to learn about Samalas.

Another volcano that caused a climate anomaly, which may have even been longer lasting than Tambora's, erupted in 536 AD. This one is not yet identified, but it could have been near Rabaul in New Guinea or even Krakatau in Indonesia. It caused famines in Europe and possibly the collapse of the Mesoamerican civilisation called Teotihuacin by promoting long droughts that led to civil unrest, famine, and war.

In 2014, Mount Kelud, a volcano in Central Java near the town of Kediri, enjoyed its tenth eruption in a century. Kelud is usually a 'moderate' volcano whose eruptions rate a three or four, and this last one was no different. However, the warning signs were read and acted on, and one hundred thousand people were evacuated from the five–kilometre exclusion zone in time, and another 100,000 people were moved at night from the ten–kilometre exclusion zone during the three–hour eruption. There were a handful of deaths when the roof of an evacuation shelter collapsed, but this compares well with Kelud's 1919 toll of five thousand victims. The news channels on TV showed the eerie scenes that falling ash creates, and we watched numerous interviews of evacuees telling of gravel and walnut–sized rocks raining down on them as they were escaping. Some, still powdered grey with ash, could have convinced a casual watcher that they were watching a black and white broadcast.

Enormous amounts of ash fell across a wide area as Kelud's ash cloud moved west over Solo and Yogyakarta, two hundred and fifty–four kilometres away and eventually out to sea. In Yogyakarta the ash that fell was reportedly only about a centimetre deep but Pak Handoko, a resident of Solo, about ninety kilometres closer, said the ash was about ten centimetres thick on his porch, and when it rained it set into a kind of slurry, like a half–set cement, heavy and sticky like clay. He said his broom was useless, and he had to dig it away with a shovel. The whole area was in chaos: schools, businesses,roads, and airports were closed, and the water and electricity system was shut down for days.

Two hundred years ago, with none of our modern knowledge of volcanology and a transport system that relied on horses or sailboats, the people on Sumbawa were hit by an eruption a thousand times bigger than Kelud. There was no community or government organised evacuation plan, and no public shelters.

They didn't stand a chance.

Chapter 3.

Life

Travelling through Sumbawa and the neighbouring islands today there is little to suggest the turmoil and difficulties of the world that Raffles knew when he was in residence in Java. These days the local people of Sumbawa and Lombok generally belong to a peaceful Muslim community, and Bali is mostly a Hindu island. People send their children to school, attend the local mosque or temple, and look forward to Sundays, or the country's numerous 'red days' (public holidays) when they shoulder one another in their haste to get to the beach, hang around a mall, or join in with family gatherings in a *warung*. There are small Christian and Balinese Hindu communities in Lombok and even smaller groups in Sumbawa, and mostly they get along well—at least for the past decade or so.

In the early nineteenth century, life was very different, and it is worth pausing to consider the local social and political scene in the time just before Tambora turned it all upside down. The nearby Balinese kingdoms (on Bali and Lombok) were regularly at war with each other or busy keeping the Dutch at bay. The peasants were called upon to pay taxes to their 'lords' and kings, serve for them as soldiers to protect their lands against coveting neighbours, or fight for them when they were in expansionist moods. Every community needed and wanted a 'lord', for without them they were vulnerable indeed. This vulnerability meant the peasants' safety and fortunes were often tied to the success of their lords and often even his or her pretentions to being a king or queen.

Klungkung is now a medium sized bustling city on the southern side of Bali but in the early eighteen hundreds, it was the 'central kingdom' of the region and the one to which all others usually deferred. Its influence ran right across Bali and Lombok and skirted the edges of Sumbawa. Except for small areas of the far western part of the island, Sumbawa's six sultanates were never actually subjugated by the Balinese, but this is not to say they weren't influenced by them.

Up to 1809, Klungkung was ruled by the war–mongering Dewa Agung Putra I. His father Sakti, known as the 'mad king of Klungkung', ended up the sole ruler when Putra was removed by having a bamboo bridge upon which he sat hacked from the sides of a ravine until he fell, presumably screaming, to a grisly death. Sakti, then an old man, allowed the management of the Klungkung kingdom to be taken over by Gusti Ayu Karan, a queen from neighbouring Karangasem. Karan it seems was an archetypical wicked–stepmother–queen whose ferocity and malevolence kept the gossip about her alive for decades, even after her death. Her main contribution to the Tambora story was setting the path for her daughter Dewa Agung Putra II to take over as the "Virgin Queen" just before the eruption. Poor Putra II happened to be in the right place at the wrong time. When the ash cloud arrived, the darkness lasted for days, and when at last it lifted there was a layer of ash more than thirty centimetres thick over everything. Roofs collapsed, wells were contaminated, and soon corpses littered the beaches and roads of her kingdom.

A landslide killed about ten thousand people in Bululeng when the ash that had piled up on a hillside gave way. Bali's whole rice crop was wiped out, and famine and disease hit the island hard for the next decade. In 1817, an epidemic killed thousands of Balinese (including the king of Badung), and in 1818 a Dutch emissary counted thirty–five corpses in the streets as he rode what must have been a very skinny horse from Badung to Gianyar. In 1821 in north Bali, a passing seaman reported numerous corpses on the beach and people trying to sell him their children so they could buy food. In 1828, thousands more died in a smallpox epidemic. Poor Queen Gusti Ayu Karan must have been at her wit's end.

So it was a period of dearth, particularly for the weaker kingdoms, but as you might expect out of any tragedy, there were opportunities for some. Lombok had been the 'rice bowl' of the region under the Balinese Karangasem kingdom since the late sixteen hundreds, and the Balinese had been able to use Lombok rice to supplement their own production for centuries. But Lombok had been hit harder than Bali by the volcanic fallout, and there was no rice available anymore. The whole crop was destroyed and soon tens of thousands died from famine and disease there too. In the wide chaos that followed the disaster, the rulers of the kingdom of Mataram took the opportunity to take over the Balinese usurpers in their land. There were six small Balinese kingdoms clustered together in the west of the island, and they were easy pickings in this time of dire straits. The new greater kingdom of Mataram rose from the ashes, literally, of Tambora.

Apart from a small incursion by the Karangasem in the west, the rulers of Sumbawa Besar and Bima had for decades successfully fought to keep the Balinese out and occasionally joined forces with sultanates from Sulawesi, vagabond groups of pirates, or mercenaries when necessary to keep it that way as much as they could. Nevertheless, Sumbawa had been under a loose yoke from the Dutch East Indies Company, the VOC, for nearly two hundred years. This yoke did not necessarily mean VOC protection from the Balinese or any of their neighbours, and the Sumbawans and Bimanese still suffered from raids that fed a flourishing slave trade.

Bali itself was a colony of the Dutch only for the thirty–six years immediately prior to the Second World War. In the seventeenth century, the Balinese enjoyed prosperity concurrent with the success of the VOC. Much of this prosperity was based on slavery and indeed, slaves were the chief export commodity of the island for many years. The kings and merchants would sell their own peasants and any they were able to capture from Lombok, Sumbawa, or other islands, as had their ancestors for eight centuries. The coming of the Dutch and the institutionalisation of slavery under law in Java brought on a golden age of prosperity for them. From Bali, slaves would go to the market in Batavia and from there across the world wherever Dutch interests lay. For a while even the French were good customers as they needed many slaves to build their colony of Bourbon in Mauritius.

Slaves were pricey commodities: in 1810, an unskilled man cost about seventy pieces of eight (around $120), a skilled labourer cost up to one hundred and fifty and women, whose price went up or down depending on their beauty and marriage prospects, ranged in price from seventy pieces of eight to one hundred and thirty. Hindu women from Bali were in demand in Batavia over Javanese as slave wives by the non–Moslem residents because they would cook and eat pork (but the Balinese kings were dealers of slaves from many islands irrelevant of religion). Sumbawan women were mostly Moslem and were desirable commodities for household staff or domestic workers. The men made good farmers, seamen, boat builders, and construction workers. They received names such as *van Samboua* and *van Bima*, and many modern day families can trace their lineage back to ancestors with names like these.

The islanders in the Tambora era must have lived in fear of slavers much of the time and were reliant on their sultans for protection. The practice was around long enough to become entrenched as a social norm for the populace and, as I mentioned, was further enhanced by the VOC "law" as it became an international trade. But socialisation would not have been much comfort for grieving families over the sudden loss through theft of one of their own, so the people tried to limit the effects of slavery and protect themselves. This is why many Sumbawan and Bimanese villages were built inland, away from the coast, where the slavers could not catch their inhabitants so easily.

Kidnapping wasn't the only route to becoming a slave. Captured soldiers often became the property of the victors as booty from a battle and would be sold afterwards. Some people ended up as slaves when they couldn't pay off debts or had a court's death sentence commuted to slavery for crimes such as black magic, theft, or murder.

Peasants who gambled excessively and lost could be taken as slaves, along with their wives and children (as women were sold with their husbands). Widowed women without male heirs would become state property and sold with any daughters as the sultan saw fit.

Slavery was also a career option of sorts. Destitute people would sell their children in times of need rather than see them starve to death, or a person so poor as to have little other choice could sell *himself* or *herself* into slavery, and the price paid would go to his or her family. He or she could then work to buy freedom. Incidentally, this is a process that still goes on today—Indonesia's labour force includes thousands of forced adult or child labourers, and the country is one of the world's largest exporters of labour. The government says that some five hundred thousand workers, over 10 per cent of the population of Lombok and Sumbawa, have left the islands to work overseas. Many become labourers or live–in housemaids and/or nannies who journey to the Middle East, Singapore, or Malaysia. Few would consider themselves slaves but some of them end up living in conditions similar to the slavery of old. We only really ever hear about them if an employer goes too far and someone dies, or a woman escapes sexual slavery and the media gets hold of the story. Desperate people are likely to put themselves at risk, and there will always be someone ready to prey on the vulnerable. Most of them, of course, make good money and bring it home to their families. In fact, it can be hard to get a flight into Lombok from other parts of Asia on an empty plane. Usually there are groups of returning workers, clutching remote controlled cars and a myriad of other souvenirs for their families, filling the seats.

As I write, *The Guardian* has reported a huge slavery problem in the Thai prawn fishing industry, with 90 per cent of the industry's three hundred thousand Burmese workers enslaved and never paid or allowed off the boats. There are rumours that some are even murdered and thrown into the sea by their Thai captains for trivial on–board offences.

The Indonesian Government regulates the labour export industry from their shores, so if the system is working properly few Indonesians will have the same problem as the Burmese sailors. Not everyone is so lucky: the International Labour Organisation says that there are 21 million men, women and children enslaved in the modern world. Perhaps little has changed in the past two centuries.

In the mid–nineteenth century, slavery was so wide spread across the East Indies it had become the norm. Even Alfred Russell Wallace, who wrote his book "*The Malay Archipelago*" only two or three years before the emancipation of slaves in 1863, accepted them lightly. He was loaned a boat and crew in Ternate to visit a nearby island, and the crew were slaves. He said, "At starting I saw something of the relation of master and slave in this part of the world." Wallace reports in detail about a group of slaves with quite some power over their master. One boatman refused to go until Wallace offered to pay him something, and on their return would not detour no matter how much cajoling was applied, as they wanted only to go home to Ternate. When they were scolded by their master for being late it was in a "bantering manner," and they "laughed and joked with him in reply." It is unlikely that many other slaves had such positive experiences.

Sumbawa is not blessed with the reliable rainfall seen in other parts of the country, such as Bali, and sometimes drought makes life hard for the population. Even in this century, it can be a surprise to discover that many people are still at severe risk of dying when things go bad. In October 2012, for instance, twenty children died of malnutrition due to the lack of rainfall and failed crops. This is hard to fathom in the twenty–first century, particularly when you learn that the West Sumbawa Regency had statistically one of the highest per capita earnings in the country in 2012 because of the Newmont Mine south of Taliwang. That it still sees starvation deaths and severe malnutrition in children is a travesty.

Chapter 4.

Preparing To Return

Since our boat trip, I had schemed and planned a number of expeditions eastwards back to Tambora, but it took a few years to sort out. My wife, The Lovely Rina, recognised from long experience that my enthusiasm for the mountain meant that I'd inevitably disappear again "into the bush" for a few days. She loves adventure too, but with our two small boys still too young to climb big mountains, she was resigned early to miss out on this one.

I did as much reading as I could about the 1815 eruption. Information online was easy to find as many web sites mention Tambora, but after reading them, they all seemed to gel together; as if their authors had researched their information from the same sources, and indeed they probably had, except that everyone seemed to have made up their own eruption death tally—anything from ninety thousand to one

hundred and fifty thousand. Because Tambora is blamed for
the 1816 *Year Without Summer,* it earns more commentary
than many other mountains, but it is still relatively unknown.

I also found a couple of excellent books on volcanoes
that had 'changed the world' and YouTube videos of people
making the climb to the rim. And the band Rasputina had
released a song called *1816, The Year Without A Summer:*

> You remember 1816 as the year without a summer.
>
> June 1816, a sudden snowstorm blankets all the countryside,
>
> So Mary Shelley had to stay inside and she wrote Frankenstein,
>
> Oh, 1816 was the year without a summer.

The two hundredth anniversary of the eruption was fast
approaching and in 2013 and 2014, it seemed that maybe
the world was waking up and getting interested. The government and tourism departments in Sumbawa were planning
to commemorate the event and raise their profile on the
international stage. Preparations were underway, and I was
invited to the 'West Nusa Tenggara–Tourism Extravaganza
Night 2013' on the thirtieth of December in a big Hotel in
Mataram. It was a free event and the more expats the better,
I was told, and I was keen to be there. It seemed someone
was getting serious about promotion, and they even had a
logo showing a stylised Tambora with '200 years' written
under it. Maybe I would meet someone who would give me
information about visiting the mountain.

A misty rain was falling as I parked my motorbike outside
the hotel and wandered into its foyer. The giant meeting and
ballrooms were easy enough to find, but I had to pick my
way through hallway renovations and a team of workers on
night–tiling duty. Inside the largest of the exhibition rooms

there were tables laden with huge metal pots of fluffy white rice and a series of *Bain–maries* with fluttering blue alcohol flames burning beneath them to warm tasty chicken and fish dishes. Hundreds of sealed disposable plastic cups of water were strategically placed like aqueous pyramids, and small groups of people milled around chatting, helping themselves to mountains of food, and sucking water through the short straws, which they had used to puncture the plastic seal of the cups.

I took a plate of food and a cup of water myself and browsed through the half dozen stalls selling knick–knacks and Lombok and Sumbawan handicrafts. There was a stall trying to sell woven shawls and blankets of brightly coloured polyester yarn, one enterprising group was marketing art T–shirts, and another selling bright plastic lampshades they'd imported from Vietnam in kit form. I'd only been there a few minutes before we were called into the ball room, and I was shown to a large round table in the front row with three or four other expats. This was to be a show for an international audience, and the Indonesians who attended were required to sit further back but, in the end, no more than a dozen expats arrived so the Indonesian guests made a rush for the empty seats at the front tables where they could sit, fidget, and help themselves to the fruit baskets left there for the absent international guests.

We watched a selection of excellent photos projected onto a big screen at the back of the stage while we waited. Lombok and Sumbawa are both photographers' dream destinations with colourful inhabitants, picturesque beaches and volcanoes, and even limestone caves.

We sat through the slide show three or four times before the VIPs arrived, two hours late, to grace us with several long winded and poorly prepared speeches in rapid Bahasa

Indonesian, losing me and most of the other expats within their first few phrases. Any festival atmosphere that may have been in the crowd at the beginning had long since evaporated, and someone wondered aloud why the entire management team of the NTB tourism authority spoke no English. This seemed odd for a state that was trying to sell themselves to the world as a tourism destination.

There was some traditional Sasak (Lombok) dancing and a fashion show of Muslim dresses. Then the announcement of several categories of tourism awards followed: Lakey Beach at Hu'u, in the Dompu Regency of Sumbawa won the coveted title of best tourist attraction.

Sadly the whole event fell flat, and a couple of sarcastic comments from the governor during his speech showed that he was not impressed either. I lasted as long as I could, but I met no one of interest and left early, bored out of my brain. On the way out, I bought a plastic lampshade shaped like a blue and white jellyfish that I didn't need because I felt sorry for the few stall owners who had expected great things of the event. One cynic told me later it was a last ditch effort to spend the government's money before year's end, and the event was just whipped together in a matter of weeks and, she said, "*Of course* Sumbawa won the awards this year, it is their turn".

I was disappointed not to find the leads into Sumbawa that I'd hoped for at the extravaganza, but a few days later The Lovely Rina told me a friend of a friend, with the curious name of Paox Iben, had heard about my interest in Tambora and was on his way to see me that afternoon. Within minutes of his arrival I had a sense that doors were beginning to open. Iben spoke slowly and clearly, which always helps me to understand Bahasa Indonesia, and he was clearly 'cool' in the old–fashioned sense, with dreadlocks he could sit on and a laid–back sauntering manner. He accepted a beer and told me he was going to ride a motorbike from Sumbawa to Europe (the trip was later scaled down to just include Asia) and back to publicise the 200th anniversary of the eruption. He called his trip *Tambora to the World* or the *Catastrophe Tour*. He showed me the 'proposal' he had written and submitted to the government and wealthy sponsors to raise the money, and he was planning to be off by April 2014. He took out the two novels he'd written and published and presented them to me, and I in turn gave him my latest book, *Turn Left at the Devil Tree.* It seemed Iben was a writer of note in Indonesia, and his upcoming trip would give him an enormous amount of material to write about. Plus, he would also be producing a film of his travels.

We studied maps of the countries he was planning to visit and discussed border crossings on a motorbike. My experience was all of thirty years old, but as I had been turned away from the Khyber Pass at the point of a machine gun, I knew a little of the challenges he was going to face. We also talked long about Sumbawa and hatched a plan. Iben said he'd like to spend his 39th birthday on the summit in five weeks' time and asked if I'd like to join him. February is still bang in the middle of the wet season, but if we had a couple of weeks' break in the monsoon, we reckoned there'd be little difficulty finding guides and getting there.

"Let's go then," he said. "Have you a motorbike?"

"Yes, of course," I replied.

My 200 cc Honda Tiger was a fine and reliable, albeit aging, machine. I had used the little road bike for touring when it was new, and still used for daily travel, but now that it was ten years old it was not what it used to be; every wet season its electrics would short out, and I knew that in February I'd still have to wait three or four months for it to dry out before using the electric starter or horn. Somehow I'd never got round to getting it fixed and had to kick start it until it dried out again.

Iben was the proud owner of a twenty–year–old 750cc Suzuki road bike in excellent condition, and he already knew the roads well. I'd have trouble keeping up with him.

Iben was also a guest curator at Mataram Museum at the time, and he was interested in culture and development of populations, drama, theatre, and history. Over the years, he'd organised several cultural festivals in a number of communities in Sumbawa. Plus, to add to his resume, he was an experienced film maker and photographer. I hoped we were going to make a good team, although what he saw of me in terms of value in our relationship I was not sure. He had contacts in Sumbawa, and even mentioned that the Sultan of Bima was an amateur historian and that we might be able to visit him. I was keen to talk to local people and discover if there were any oral histories about the eruption still told in the villages. Iben would be able to talk with people much more fluently than I and be able to translate into clear Bahasa Indonesian if I had problems understanding people's accents or the local Sumbawanese dialect. Iben hoped to practise his English with me too, as he knew it would be a useful language for him to have on his travels.

An old mate from Australia contacted me and wanted to join us. Hughen McConaghy and I had met in Alice Springs nearly thirty years earlier, and over the years, we had made several interesting journeys together in outback Australia, climbing mountains in New Zealand, or diving on the Great Barrier Reef. Hughen's plan was to hire a bike in

Lombok and come along to Tambora. I was happy because we were both much older than the last time we had climbed mountains, and I thought maybe I'd need him to push me.

Iben called me during January and invited us to the opening of an exhibition he was organising at the Mataram Museum about Bungin Island, which lies just off the coast of Sumbawa. I'd never heard of Bungin Island before.

"It's in Sumbawa," he said. "The most densely populated island in the world."

I checked the map, and it wasn't even marked. How could that be? A secret Island? My curiosity rose, and on the next night, we packed the kids into the car and drove to Mataram Museum. We were late, but as the Governor was going to open the exhibition with a speech, I wasn't too concerned about missing the beginning. But he was even later than we were, and people were sitting in rows of white plastic chairs eating cakes and snacks out of cardboard boxes waiting for him. It seems an unwritten rule that the more important a person is in Indonesia, the longer the people have to wait.

Iben was there already; stressed by the lateness of the governor and busy checking for the hundredth time that everything was ready. I took my sons into the old part of the museum where they could see swords and a few dioramas of village life, complete with half–sized plastic fishermen throwing half–sized nets. There was a case of local butterflies and a locked room with a glass door through which we could see a few gold plated pots and *keris* knives in display cases. When music started, we went back out to watch a troupe of athletic Sumbawan dancers demonstrating their skills. Sumbawan traditional dance, I noticed, contrasts markedly with the slow moving precise motions of Lombok's dancing. It was athletic with excellent rhythmic music on drums and the traditional windpipes known as *basarune* playing the tunes.

I hadn't seen The Lovely Rina for a while, but suddenly she was back from wherever she had been.

"I've been talking to the old men from Bungin in the exhibition. Come and meet them."

We left the dancers and crossed to the as–yet–unopened exhibition. Inside three old men were sitting on bamboo mats surrounded by their instruments. They had been waiting there for hours for the exhibition to open so they could play their tunes and welcome the visitors. Rina introduced the two she had been talking to. Bapaks Yusef and Marhain were both fine old gentlemen in their eighties, and they'd been brought here to perform in the exhibition. A number of young girls hovered about them, dressed in traditional finery, no doubt having a dual role as part of the exhibition, but also caring for the old men. We talked about Bungin Island—apparently, it was hardly an island at all. Just after the eruption of Tambora, it was a coral quay that rose above the water at high tide that the fishermen used to use to dry their nets. The first settlers arrived in 1818, three years after the eruption, so it had had nearly two hundred years of growth and improvement. In 2002, for example, the island was only six hectares in size, but these days it is more than eight. "Why is that?" I asked Pak Marhain.

"Because there are more people now. We have a custom. If a man wants to get married, he has to make more land and build his house on it. The men gather coral rubble and just build the land. There are nearly four thousand people who live there, on eight hectares. It's the highest population density of any island in the world."

I did some mental maths—each person would have about twenty square metres, about the size of my bedroom at home.

Bapak Marhain said that he was a descendent of the man who had first settled the island. "Five generations," he said. Marhain's ancestor had been a 'general' who led people there to build houses and start the new community. I thought it was interesting that he knew this because many Indonesians have little idea of their family's history. The Lovely Rina's Sundanese family of five, for instance, don't share the same surname, and all their aunts and uncles and most other elderly people are called *Tante* or *Om* (Uncle or Aunt). Personal names are rarely, if ever, used or even known among her extended family unless people are particularly close. Many Indonesians like President Suharto for instance, only have one name, making genealogy a more challenging pursuit. Another cultural difference I have noticed in my extended family is that people don't remember or celebrate each other's birthday, and if an individual wants to do so, it is their job to tell everyone what day it is, not for the others to remember. The Lovely Rina, for example, would never be sent birthday cards by an aunt or her brother or sisters unless she asked for them.

There was a large stuffed crocodile as part of the exhibition. It was at least four metres long and sat on the floor with stiff, swollen limbs and glass eyes ablaze amid pots and fishing nets, a harpoon spear, a few pieces of cloth, and some woven baskets. The *bapaks* wanted photos sitting beside it with my boys, Harry and Roy, so together they posed with the giant reptile, looking puny beside its frozen jaws. The girls wanted photos standing with me, another giant in this land, so I obliged. Being two metres tall I towered over the tiny girls, and I managed to hold a cheesy grin for a few minutes while they took pictures with their smartphones.

"Do you still have crocodiles at Bungin?" I asked the old men. "Not since the 1960s," Yusef said. "This one is very old. I can remember him swimming. We just have goats now". Crocodiles used to be numerous, and they still are in remote parts of South East Asia, including eastern Indonesia, but they are mostly gone in the more settled areas. News reports of fisherman getting eaten by crocodiles in West Papua still occasionally appear.

I looked up Bungin Island later that night and discovered that these days in Indonesia, the island is most famous for what the goats eat. Journalists have been excited to learn from enthusiastic boat drivers that there is no grass or other plants on the island, and the large population of goats survive eating rags, paper, and plastic. The *Jakarta Post* had a full page Sunday special on this diet and talked of it as a major tourist attraction and even tour agencies wax lyrical about the nutrition of goats. One claimed that the human population was the densest in the world at fourteen thousand per square kilometre—I thought those poor people must have to take it in turns to sit down—perhaps they have to sit on the goats. The *Jakarta Post* article was so upbeat about Bungin Island; I expected we would find a ticket office, souvenir stands, ice cream sellers, and regular tourist boats across to it filled with busloads of camera toting, goat loving *parawisata* from Java. The reality proved a little different.

Bungin Islanders belong to a tribal group called Bajo. The Bajo are famous as sea gypsies, who live on boats or stilt houses across a wide part of South East Asia. The original Bungin Island families came here to avoid harassment from the *Samawa* (now known as Sumbawa) tribe on the mainland. They built stilt houses on a reef of broken coral that was exposed only at high tide, all with their backs to the sea, and they stacked more coral rubble around them to give them dry land. They were only a few hundred metres off shore, but this gave them security, and they stayed, trading fish and sea–cucumbers called *trepang* with the mainlanders for tools and rice. They collected firewood from, and buried their dead on, a real island further west, and the system seemed to work well.

Until recently, the community remained tight and closed to the outside world: they spoke their own language (*Bahasa Bajo* is closely related to Tagalog from the Philippines*)* and cloistered their girls until marriage. However, these days they have mobile phones, electricity, and a school that teaches in Bahasa Indonesian, and they have largely joined the rest of Indonesian society, for better or worse.

We left the old men when we could hear the Governor speaking to the gathering outside and because it was getting late for our kids, but I promised that I would visit Bungin Island soon and bring copies of the photos I had taken.

During the next few weeks, I had my motorbike serviced and continued to gather information, raring to go. Hughen arrived a few days early, and then Iben delayed our departure for a day because of work commitments, but he did manage to track down a friend who would rent out his Kawasaki 150cc trail bike to Hughen. Then, Iben's contacts in Sumbawa reported that we were unlikely to be able to climb the mountain safely as it was very wet and hidden in cloud most of the time. None of us had any desire to slip and slide through mud to go up a volcano to see nothing but cloud, so we changed our plans and delayed the climb till the dry season. There would be plenty of other things to see in Sumbawa.

On a fine Wednesday morning, we packed up the motorbikes, waved goodbye to The Lovely Rina, and

headed east. It had taken Iben several hours to collect the
motorbike from his friend for Hughen, so we didn't actually
get going until after lunch. We then spent several less–than–
entertaining hours in the Lombok traffic sorting out our
travel protocols—Hughen sped on passed us at a petrol
station without being seen and ended up fifty kilometres
ahead while we looked for him and continually tried to reach
him by phone. When he finally answered he was nearly at
the ferry port and had to wait for us. Then, when I caught
up, I didn't see him or Iben and rode right past and straight
to the ferry. Confusion reigned for a while, but we all got
there together eventually.

We had ridden through much of the country explored
in 1856 by Alfred Russell Wallace, the naturalist who was
a co–author with Charles Darwin of the theory of natural
selection. In his book, *The Malay Archipelago,* he described
this area well. Lombok, in those days, was a very different
land, and the countryside was now not so wild–people are
less likely to be stabbed by a *keris* and left for dead; there
are no violent all–powerful sultans, and the population has
exploded. These days just a very few patchy remnants of
undisturbed forest exist in central Lombok, although nature
still rules for much of the highlands, and some of the southern coastal area is reasonably untouched. Wallace described
the vegetation as "stunted and thorny" and complained that
it was very hard for him to catch insects or retrieve the birds
he shot. He never went to Sumbawa, but interestingly he
says that the "natives" of Lombok claimed the prickles and
thorns of Lombok were "nothing" compared to those of
Sumbawa, whose surface still bore "the covering of volcanic
ashes thrown out forty years ago by the terrible eruption of
Tambora." Perhaps this was why he never went there.

The prickles and thorns weren't going to deter us, however. We bought our 53,000 rupiah tickets for the Sumbawa ferry crossing in high spirits. Car ferries in Indonesia connect every major island twenty–four hours a day. The port of Labuhan Lombok links Lombok with Poto Tano on Sumbawa, and the ferries generally take an hour and a half to make the crossing. Nonetheless, we had to wait an hour for ours to arrive while a light rain started to fall. Everyone with motorbikes parked them together in a close group on one side and huddled under trees or the roof of the guardroom, whilst the cars and trucks lined up in an orderly fashion on the other, their drivers peering through their wet windscreens, smoking quietly.

It was far from busy; there were no more than thirty bikes. But after unloading the cars, bikes, and passengers coming the other way, the boatmen opened their gates for those of us waiting to board, and there was suddenly a mad dash with everyone trying to get on first. Like the others, we pushed and shoved in the crowd, as if there was limited space, and we were afraid of being too late to get on board. In the end, we could have played tennis on the empty space on the car deck.

The rain stopped, and we sat on benches on the roof in the fading afternoon light as the boat headed east. All was good with the world. We bought tiny portions of *nasi goreng*, fried rice in banana leaf wrapping, at inflated prices and started to relax, and I phoned The Lovely Rina and our boys to let them know our progress.

As a foreigner in Indonesia, you get used to locals noticing you and being the centre of attention. Often people come up and ask where you are from and where you are going, if you are married, and how many kids you have. So, when a sad–faced man with big, rubbery, downturned lips came and sat opposite me, I wasn't surprised when he started to question me; I was ready with the usual stock answers.

"Where are you from?" he asked. "Australia," I replied.

"Not you," he said. He pointed at Iben who was standing leaning against the rail, his metre length dreadlocks blowing in the wind like Medusa at a party. "*Him!*"

Chapter 5.

Four Year Old Jockeys.

We were so late on arrival in Sumbawa, Iben changed our plans. There are no commercial guesthouses or hotels near Poto Tano but because he knew the *kepala desa* (the village headman) of a small town only twenty minutes ride east, he knew we would be able to stay there. I had probably offended a *kepala desa* before when I had entered a village and accidentally asked to speak with the *kelapa desa*, the village coconut, so I decided to be on my best behaviour.

His wooden house was on the waterfront in Labuhan Mapit, and like all the others, it had its back to the sea, and its front doors opened into the community. Labuhan Mapit was the fishing village where Iben had spent time organising a festival about a year before. Everyone was friendly, and we were welcomed with open arms. A neighbour came in and berated Iben good naturedly for not giving her warning and time to prepare, but then she set off to find some fish for dinner. She returned after a few minutes saying there was no fish, but she had plenty of squid, *cumi cumi*, and we'd eat that instead.

The *kepala desa* was a family man named Alvin who was in his fifties. He had two teenage children, a son and a daughter, and they were literally surrounded by other relatives because Alvin was one of nine brothers, and five of them lived within a stone's throw. He had been the elected *kepala desa* for many years and seemed well liked by everyone.

The squid was barbequed on a small fire outside, and we ate it with rice and their local version of the fiery chilli paste found everywhere in Indonesia named *sambal*. Iben managed to find a few warm bottles of beer, and we sat outside around the fire chatting until bedtime.

Hughen was given a mattress in a hot little room at the front of the house whilst I managed to stretch out on the couch in the *kamar tamu*, the reception room always found at the front of Indonesian houses. Because I asked him, Alvin brought me an electric fan which I enjoyed for several hours until Hughen stole it and put it in his room. He had laid in a pool of sweat, unable to sleep in his fan–less hotbox, and to hear me snoring away in total comfort was too much to bear.

I rose very early and wandered around the village a little to look at the houses. They were invariably made of wood and most were on stilts, with wooden steps climbing to their front verandas. Alvin's house was ground level and appeared more solid than the others, but perhaps that is fitting for the head of the village.

The sea behind the houses was walled off. There was no beach, but rocks had been piled up against the wall, and every few meters there was a wooden stepladder that allowed easy access over the wall to small jetties. Several small fishing boats were anchored in the shallows. A sour smell of old fish hung in the air, reminiscent of most fishing villages I had visited.

The others roused themselves, and after we'd drunk sweet black coffee so thick we could nearly stand a spoon up in it, we left Alvin's house and headed east for an hour or so to a town with the unfortunate name of Alas, dragged from the depths of despair by being pronounced 'Alice'. Alas was bustling. It is a market town and many horse carts were lined up against the market ready to take shoppers home with their goods.

We pushed through the crowds on the road, passed through Alas quickly, and soon turned off the highway onto an unmarked dirt road that headed towards Bungin Island. After meeting the old men from Bungin at the museum several weeks before and reading all the media hype about the weird diet their goats have and how tightly people are packed onto a coral reef, I was a little disappointed to find the real Bungin a little different to the village I had built in my mind. The first surprise was that these days there was now a causeway across the shallow sea reaching the village, and we rode onto the island along a broad access road at about eight in the morning. Kids wearing the red shorts or dresses and white shirts of the country's elementary schools were heading off to their morning classes. Large numbers of women were sitting on plastic chairs or wooden benches in the shade of their houses, watching their toddlers play on the dirt streets. The houses are packed closely together and many are on stilts so that the space under them becomes a living room or work area. We parked beside the house of one of one of Iben's friends, and we were introduced. Some surly youths were sleeping on the floor, and they rose, grumbling, and disappeared into the house to continue their rest.

Hughen, who among other things, farms goats in Australia, checked out the healthy narrow–hipped Bungin variety of goats and marvelled at how tame they were.

"Can't see any eating any rags, though," he complained. "Maybe they've run out," I replied.

We went for a walk through the village. It is pretty in a medieval sort of way; with small shops under some of the houses opening directly onto the street and steep wooden staircases rising to meet small doors about two metres off the ground. In one of the shops, a couple of goats were helping themselves to some candy, plastic wrappers and all.

"See, it's true!" I pointed. "No it's not, look there."

Several goats were eating the husks and leaves of sugar cane plants a woman had just thrown to them. They were vegetarians after all. Later, we did see one small goat chewing on the arm of a newly washed shirt left hanging on a string outside someone's house but that was hardly weird enough to write a full page article about for a national newspaper.

Iben's friend explained that when a man wants to marry, he has to build more land for his house, so the island grows bigger with the population. Two other people also mentioned this to me within a ten minute time period. It was interesting and may well be true, but I was getting the feeling it was a marketing ploy. Maybe the *kepala desa* has gathered everyone and said, "Now, whatever you do, if you get the chance, tell tourists that the goats eat rags and grooms have to build more land." Everyone would have nodded obediently and set off to find some unsuspecting outsider to educate. Or maybe everyone had read the *Jakarta Post* article.

Still, the people were very friendly and a pleasure to visit. We were asked to photograph babies and even had to pose with some, and once we were shown a large fresh octopus a woman had on ice under her house. We stopped for a coffee outside a small *warung,* and a few mothers gathered to entertain their babies. And what a lot of babies there were! We saw few of their fathers—perhaps they were away fishing for the day, but there were many, many small children.

"It looks like they are ensuring their claim to the title of most highly populated island in the world is safe for a while," I said.

Unfortunately, Bapaks Yusef and Marhain were not in Bungin, and as it's only a small place, after our little wander around and the coffee, we moved on.

We were back on the bikes only a short while when we stopped for breakfast. We quickly were learning that Iben had a knack of finding, or deep insider knowledge, about the best places to eat. This restaurant, or *rumah makan*, was an unprepossessing concrete building among many along the road, and normally I wouldn't even have noticed it as I went by, but we breakfasted extremely well on coffee, small, deep fried fish, and corn patties with rice. Suddenly, Iben groaned as he remembered a bag he'd left back in Bungin, and Hughen and I had to wait for him in the restaurant. We had another excellent coffee, and when at last he returned, we continued eastwards and followed the coast for a while. At one point, I looked back and could see Bungin stretched out across an impossibly flat sea—there wasn't a breath of wind to even ruffle its surface. Bungin was a cluster of houses, with a tall dome of a mosque standing above them, and thirty or forty kilometres behind it; dwarfing everything was the huge grey muscular shape of Mount Rinjani on Lombok, reminding us that in Indonesia you are never very far away from a volcano.

We continued east along the highway and discovered it to be often tree-lined in these parts with *Trimbisi* trees meeting in the middle of the road, creating a tunnel. Their shade was much appreciated as the day was already hot. After a few hours, we passed straight through the edge of Sumbawa Besar, the capital of the western two thirds of Sumbawa and the second largest city on the island after Bima, with about sixty thousand inhabitants.

Iben was keen to get to some horse races called *kerato* he had heard were happening near a village named Penyaring. Many villages in Sumbawa have *kerato*. They are keen to maintain them as a traditional sport, and this would be our chance to see one. We stopped at a local market, and Iben asked several men hanging around their horse carts for directions. They were poor informants because they told us completely the wrong way, and we ended up getting bushwhacked for an hour or so on really rough dirt roads. After asking a few, more reliable, people, we finally regained the sealed road, passed between some marginal–looking dried out rice paddies, and entered a plain of dry open country with rows of thorny bushes lining the roads to act as fences for stock.

The horse race track we were looking for was at the end of the road, and it was clearly a permanent fixture. It had a large stand, which would cater for at least a thousand spectators watching over a broad, fenced, racetrack. About three hundred metres to the left of the stand were the starting gates, and to the right, the track ran straight for another two or three hundred metres before the first curve. Then it continued the circle to rejoin the straight near the starting gate. The horses would run the full circle to the finish line next to the race caller's box. Behind the stand, spread over a couple of hectares, we could see the temporary camps of the horsemen and their families. There were blue tarpaulins stretched between wooden posts where horses were tethered beside rough tents that their handlers slept in. Several trucks were pulled up, and there was a row of *warung* where people could buy cold drinks, noodles, and even substantial meals. A large excavation in the middle of this area was full of rain water, and one man was gently washing his horse with the muddy water.

The sweet smell of the horses was pleasantly familiar. This was going to be just like a country race meeting back home.

We parked the bikes amid hundreds of others. Iben's eyes were lit up with photographer's glee, and it was clear his itchy shutter finger was ready to work. He led us right across the front of the stand, and the five hundred or so punters went quiet as we paraded by. We made an odd sight—I guess—Iben's dread locks and my two metre height were probably rare sights at their races, and Hughen and I were the only *bule* there.

"Can we bet, Iben? Are there bookies here?" Hughen was enthusiastic. "Sure you can," Iben replied and began to look as if he was about to arrange it.

"No, not really," said Hughen. "I don't know anything about these horses. I don't want to bet."

The crowd wasn't unfriendly but nor were they inviting. Gambling is officially illegal in Indonesia, so I suspected they weren't keen on having outsiders visit. The bookies were clandestine and part of the crowd in the stand. People would cluster around them before and after races so thickly that it was impossible to see if there was money changing hands or not.

They were friendlier up at the finish line. Within minutes, the announcer had invited Hughen and I to climb up into his calling box, and we were put in uncomfortable plastic chairs to watch the races.

"You, tourists, come up. You can see? Pak, give him that chair. Ooh, very tall. Where do you come from? Australia, ah, good," he said, which was nice of him, though he never took the microphone from his lips, and his voice boomed out of twenty loud speakers. The entire crowd knew where we were and shared any information he could glean from us.

Already a little awed by the event in a 'what–the–hell–is–happen–ing–here?' kind of way before we'd climbed up to the box, we had first walked up to the gate where the horses and jockeys are led off after their race. The horses in the first race had come thundering by but one had played up and thrown his red shirted jockey off headfirst into the wooden fence just near me and he had lain face down, inert in the dust. I wondered at neck injuries or concussion and expected someone would assess any damage, but one of the horse trainers just rushed to him and picked him up roughly and shook him.

"Bloody hell!" I said. "I hope he's not hurt—he'll end up in a wheel chair." The jockey was carried back to the gate, and he had come round and was able to stand. It was then I realised how small he was. He had a black knitted face mask on, like a wayward bank robber, but when someone took it off, I saw he was a child and very young at that. By this time the other horses had been stopped by men waving strips of cloth and getting in their way. The jockeys had finished their race and they were led through the gate. All of them were small children.

"They're just kids," I said.

"Well, they're only small horses," Hughen replied. He was right. They were Sumbawa ponies, only 11 or 12 hands high. Immensely strong and willing, their breed is renowned as excellent stock, and they pull carts around communities throughout the island. They descend from Mongolian and other Chinese breeds, though there are stories of ponies being brought by the Dutch from South Africa to the neighbouring island of Sumba hundreds of years ago, so it is possible they also share an African bloodline. Of the eight Indonesian breeds of horses, Sumbawa and Sumba ponies are famed for their strength and stamina. All the horses in the races were stallions, and there was a range of colours—chestnut, black, gray and dun, and *orange*. Hughen spotted the orange stallion on a lunging rope out the back, warming up, and yes indeed, he was bright orange. I had a closer look at him later, and I suspect he was dyed, but it was very hard to tell.

We had lost sight of Iben, but as a photographer, he was in his element, so we let him do his thing, and we decided to wander down to the starting gates and watch there for a while. It was fenced off by bamboo partitions, but when we came close, a short fat man dressed in army fatigues, with the name Mochamad embroidered across his shirt in large capital letters, called us over and opened the fence so that we could join him. He was indeed a soldier, and he and a couple of his mates were moonlighting in their army fatigues as security. Some horses were being led down for the next race, and several jockeys were already there, perched on the railings inside the starting gate. A couple of other boys were being carried on the backs of the trainers, or perhaps their fathers, down to join them.

A very small boy was put on a dancing chestnut stallion where he held on tightly to a thick halter rope around the horse's neck. I asked him how old he was. All I could see through his black knitted face mask were his eyes and the thin lips of his mouth. He just looked at me. I asked the man holding his horse.

"Four," he replied. The jockey was four years old!

I found Mochamad. "Are all these jockeys still so young?"

"Yes," he replied. "They can be four, five, or six years old. By seven, they are too big for the horse." A short career, then on the scrap heap at seven! I thought of my own four year old son in Junior Prep at school in Lombok. I wasn't comfortable with the concept of four year old jockeys.

"Do they like it?" I asked. "They're very young."

"Yes, of course," he replied, looking at me strangely for finding it unusual. "Now come here, down like this. You can get a good photo here."

Obediently, I squatted down beside the fence with my camera. Hughen had placed himself right beside the starting gate, so when it opened, he was in a good position to get photos of the horses' first burst of acceleration. The gate was a metal screen which was pulled down like a garage door and spring loaded. The race would start when the spring was released, and the gate swung up. The tension rose as the last horse was put into his stall, nose against the gate. The horses knew it was race time and were raring to go. The whips that landed on their rumps by the trainers wound them up and left them in no doubt what was to come. I looked through my camera, tense with expectation. There was a shout. I pressed my shutter button, the gate was up, and the horses were off, the boys holding grimly to their halters as they disappeared down the straight.

I checked my photo—a nice shot of skinny horse legs beneath the barely opened gate. I'd have to try again.

The horses came round the bend. The boys were no longer

gripping their necks but sitting upright, one hand in the mane and the other whipping the horses to ever increasing speed. They were poetry in motion, undoubtedly skilled riders. The race was fast and furious, but by no means equal with several lengths between the winning horse and the others.

The loud speakers called out the winners: "Two, three, and five." Number two was a six year old in green. He was the only boy who smiled at us or acknowledged our presence the whole time we were there—clearly a confident and experienced rider. "Go green!" I yelled in a later race. He asked me to take his photo, proud of his skill.

"Where do you get these horses?" I asked Mochamad.

"They come from Bima," he said. "All the good horses come from there. They bring them by truck. Look." Going passed us was a small, open–backed truck with a horse standing quietly in its tray, tethered to bars on the cabin. It was certainly passive and well trained. Two men were sitting on the side rails smoking.

Hughen was again lying down next to the start, his camera poised. The trainers were ushering the next set of horses, including the odd–looking orange horse we had spotted earlier, into the stalls. Some of the boys were rubbing mud onto the inside of their trousers to increase their grip. None of them used saddles.

"Isn't it dangerous? Does anyone ever get hurt?"

"No not here," said Mochamad. "In Bali, there were races and a Japanese tourist tried lying on the track to get a photograph. The horses jumped at this, they were scared. One boy was thrown off and killed. Not here though."

"I don't think four year old kids in Australia would ever be allowed to do this," I commented.

"No, but here in Sumbawa they are crazy," said Mochamad.

"Oh. Where do you come from?" I asked him.

"Sumbawa," he grinned. "I am crazy too."

We watched a few more races. A marshal with a clipboard was organising the horses, and I asked him how many races there were.

"Many more," he replied, flipping through several pages. I could see the racing would be continuing into the evening.

"There are buffalo races near here soon, only ten kilometres away," Mochamad told me. "You can join in. For one hundred thousand rupiah you can ride."

Buffalo races in Indonesia are an interesting challenge. The skill comes in steering two buffaloes through the mud of a rice paddy towards a stick in the mud and to run that stick over. The 'jockeys' at these races stand on a wooden frame like a bladeless plough tied between the two buffaloes and which they drag behind at speed. It takes practice, good balance, an understanding of buffaloes, and not a little courage. They occur at the beginning of rice planting season because the races are actually held in the paddies. Riders get soaked to the skin and covered in mud, and it seems a lot of fun. There's a bit of cheating that can go on, of course. In the case of buffalo races, the buffaloes can be reluctant runners, and the word is in Lombok that they run a lot faster if their owners smear the inside of the animals' rectums with fresh pulped chilli juice. Perhaps they did that here too.

We left Mochamad and the boys to find Iben. He was a happy man who'd already taken several hundred photos, and after "just one more race," which turned into two or three, we finally packed up to leave. We still had several hundred kilometres to go to Empang, where we were to spend the night.

Chapter 6.

From Jellyfish To Mountain

Trails

The town of Empang is a few kilometres inland of the southern shore of Saleh Bay. Like most small Indonesian roadside towns, it extended along the highway but only two or three blocks deep on either side. Iben led us off the road down a narrow lane and parked at the gate of a beautiful garden. Our host was another of Iben's friends, Pak Marban—a sociology teacher at the local high school and an expert at bonsai. His delightful garden was full of beautifully prepared bonsai trees of at least six different species. He has three children, and he was delighted to welcome us into his home. We drank coffee with him in the *berugaq* (an outside sitting platform with a roof similar to the Balinese *bale*) while his wife, whose name I never learned, was busy in the kitchen.

A small handsome man wearing the white *topi* of a haji joined us and was introduced as Haqqul Amin. He spoke English well and taught it in the local high school, and Marban had called him and invited him over to practice his English with us. A thin wispy beard hung from his chin, and he was impeccably dressed, wearing a white 'topi' hat traditionally worn by Muslims who had completed their pilgrimage, or *haj,* to Mecca. Haqqul told me he came from a family of fisherman and three of his brothers had boats. They all lived in the village of Labuhan Jambu, about ten kilometres further on, and he knew Saleh Bay well. He had been across to the Tambora side of the bay many times by boat. "We get all our sand for building over there." "Have you been on a *haj*, Pak?" I asked looking at his *topi*.

"No," he replied. "The white *topi* is just the fashion. These days anyone can wear one."

I asked him if there were any stories about the 1815 eruption passed down through his family. "No," he said. "It was too long ago." This was what I heard everywhere I went and people in Lombok and in the west of Sumbawa had even said that Tambora was too far away and hadn't affected their ancestors at all, although I knew that large numbers of the casualties came from both these areas. Clearly the "living memory" I was hoping for was not going to be easy to find. British reports at the time had stated that people in Sumbawa experienced heavier ash falls than on the Bima side, and they were selling their buffalos and horses, which they couldn't feed, for a "half or quarter rupees worth of rice and corn." Some communities in Sumbawa were eventually relieved for a short time by an aid ship which brought "sixty–three coyangs of rice" from Java, but up to fifty per cent of the Sumbawan population were either killed outright by the eruption or tsunamis, starved to death, or died of disease. Many more left and went to other islands to sell themselves into slavery (see chapter three).

Raffles had abolished the large Batavia slave market in 1813 and was attempting to stamp out the practice throughout the archipelago. Selling oneself or children into slavery seems savage these days, but for centuries, it had been a viable economic option for survival during famines and desperate times. So, Raffle's good work in trying to abolish slavery ironically cut off one of the few traditional options for desperate people, and there was no doubt that further deaths occurred because of it during the famine. In Bali, there are stories of parents killing their children on the beaches, unable to sell them and unwilling to watch them starve.

Changing the subject, I asked Haqqul about the jellyfish I had seen in Labuhan Sangoro two years before, and he said that his village was the other major collection point for the trade on this coast.

"Jellyfish are a good business, but we don't eat them. They go to China," he said. "My brothers stop fishing for fish during the season and start collecting them because they get more money. We rent a room to the Chinese buyer—he cannot speak either Indonesian or English, so he's very quiet. He comes every year for three months." Haqqul described how the fishermen were paid by the volume of jellyfish they caught, so there was a knack to scooping them out of the water and keeping them wet and therefore full size. The season lasts only three months, from November to January, and it is a reasonably young industry, having started here in 2008.

"The jellyfish come up out of deep water in November. Before we caught them, they used to wash up dead on the beaches in large numbers and really stink. It's not so bad now."

"Why do they only take the middle part of the jellyfish and not the bell?" I asked.

"They tried to take the bell in the beginning, but for this species, it's too soft and didn't work. They wash the heads, add *tawas* (alum) to the water to get the dirt out, then salt the heads and get a tough gel. It's the women's job to do the salting and to pack them into the drums for transport."

Nobody really knows why the jellyfish come up to the surface like they do. Haqqul said that one year they came so close to the shore in Labuhan Jambu that children went out to catch some. Jellyfish seem to like the rain and come right to the surface, but they stay a little way down if the sun is too bright, so they are easier to catch in the early morning and afternoon. By February, they are either dead or gone again, and the fishermen return to more traditional fishing.

February is the windy month of the monsoon, and the bay gets very rough. "There are two types of fishing. Net fishing is called *bagang* and line fishing is *begoh*. In February, it is too rough for nets, so they can only use lines."

Haqqul went home soon after, but not until he'd given us a warm invitation to stay in Labuhan Jambu next time we passed through.

Hughen and I were set up to sleep in an empty room, and Iben slept outside in the *barugaq* under a mosquito net. Poor Iben, who found it hard to sleep at the best of times, hadn't gone to sleep until after two, but at five thirty I was already shaking him awake. Our plan had been to ride all the way to Pancasila on the slopes of Tambora and back out again, so an early start was essential.

One of the things that Haqqul had talked about the night before was corn. The coast around Jambu is magnificent agricultural country, and the road passes through whole valleys of corn farms. Haqqul told me that this area is second only to Sulawesi for corn.

"How do you eat it here?" I asked.

"We don't much," he replied. "It's all for export. It all goes to China like the jellyfish. Three years ago the vice president came with a delegation from China. They promised they were going to build a corn port, but we're still waiting."

Riding the road through the corn farms was pleasant. The land undulates and it appeared the hills and valleys had a giant striped green blanket smothering them for many kilometres. The corn was planted very close together, which is a testament to the rich fertile soil produced by the volcanoes of the region. It is ironic that the initially toxic and clogging volcanic ash deposits, which have high levels of rhyolite and biotite, break down to help produce some of the most fertile soils in the world and become a tremendous agricultural boon to farmers. This takes many years and in Sumbawa there were at least ten years of famine after the eruption. (Famines were not unknown as a normal part of life in these parts of Indonesia. Lombok, for instance recorded eleven years of famine in the twentieth century even without volcanic eruptions, the last in 1976—77. The worst Lombok famine of that century occurred in 1965—66 with ten thousand and fifty–three people dying.)

We stopped for breakfast at a restaurant on a small beach. It was clear that the weather hit this end of the bay full on because, on the beach, driftwood and pumice had piled high among the stones. Much of it was beautifully sculpted by the sea. There was enough timber here to build several houses, and I imagined what it must have been like here two centuries earlier. After the eruption, raft islands of pumice and trees pushed into the sea by pyroclastic flows and tsunamis were everywhere in Saleh Bay and the seas north and west of Tambora. Some of the rafts were more than five kilometres long, and ships could get stuck in them for days. This beach would have been piled very high, and the open water may have been kilometres away.

After leaving the restaurant, we followed the road as it climbed and wrapped around several steep cliffs. The surface was broad and well made, and despite occasional patches of gravel on the bends which created a slipping hazard, and the odd corner with a peculiar camber that threatened to tip us over the edge, it was an excellent motor bike ride. There was little traffic, and what was there was all slow moving and easy to pass anyway. What motorcyclist does not like a good mountain road? Hughen on his Kawasaki looked about as happy as a man could be on a motor bike. I told him so.

"You bet," he replied. "This is fantastic, the best way to travel."

We reached a T–junction in a town named Soriutu. Iben had organised another friend to meet him here, and he was already on his way, so we had a break from the bikes and a short wait in the shade of a *warung*. We had entered the Dompu regency which surrounds the regional capital of the same name.

I knew that after the eruption, Raffles dispatched Lieutenant Owen Philips to this area, which he called 'Dompo'. He brought some emergency rice and supplies to some of the survivors and reported on the aftermath of the eruption in Dompu. He described absolute desolation from the ash, poisoned water and diseased, starving, homeless people (see chapter six). These days Soriutu is a dusty vibrant market town. While we waited, several trucks laden with garlic and other crops went east towards Bima, and in the back of a pickup truck we saw a pair of white cattle standing quietly as they passed through town, resigned to their fate. I watched a woman struggling with a trevally fish more than a meter long—she was trying to tie it securely to her motor scooter but finding it unwieldy and slippery.

We didn't have to wait long. Within minutes, two young men arrived on a motorbike. Subhan, an agricultural engineer based in Bima, and his mate named Son, a sports education student, had ridden across from Bima that morning to join us on our Tambora adventure. Iben introduced us, and without any further delay, we started heading west to see the mountain.

The road wound down from the Dompu plain towards the sea. We passed through a few towns and villages, which were surrounded by paddies, corn farms, and fruit trees. The ash fall here had been heavy, up to fifty centimetres thick. Lieutenant Philips had reported that, "The trees and herbage... had been completely destroyed." It was difficult to imagine this rich farmland a grey wasteland of ash.

The atmosphere was very hazy, as it had been for a week or more, so we hadn't yet sighted Tambora. However, soon the road entered a verdant open savannah, which grazing animals had close cropped. Stands of thorny acacia trees were haphazardly spreading across the gently undulating land. Occasionally steep–walled gullies slashed the slopes northwards by several kilometres, and there, above them, we could pick out the dark shadow of Tambora through the haze. It was still early, but the clouds were gathering, and within minutes of our first sighting, the mountain was lost to view once again.

This is cattle country and herds of white cattle grazed across the grassland. Many wore bells around their necks, and all moved with their personal clouds of little black flies, which settled in great numbers around their eyes.

There were also buffaloes, and we saw large herds wallowing in mud right next to the beach; their ears flicking away the annoying insects as they passively chewed their cud as I climbed down to them to take photographs. They ignored me completely—the Asian water buffalo is a docile beast in Asia, but this same species lives feral in Australia's Northern Territory and is so dangerous it has been known to kill people. In most of Southeast Asia, it has an important role as a traditional beast of burden with a significant farming role, as well as an excellent source of meat. For indigenous people like the Toraja from South Sulawesi, buffalos are an integral part of a very complex and fascinating culture.

A few kilometres of rough dirt road tested our bikes. At one point, my chain fell off, and we stopped for a short time in the village of Hodo, where a mechanic tightened it for me. The road was mostly good thereafter, and we followed the coast northwest to the town of Calabai, where we bought fruit and a type of filled pancake called *matabak* for lunch. Then we turned east and started to climb the lower slopes of the mountain towards Pancasila.

The vegetation changed again. Larger trees and coffee plantations became the norm. The coffee plants were fruiting but not yet ripe. I later hunted around for any ripe fruit (which contains the bean) because I have heard it is quite delicious and worth eating, but I was disappointed to find none ready.

Pancasila—a small village that bills itself as the gateway to Tambora, sits on the boundary of Dompu and Bima provinces. From here, the trail starts for a two–day hike to the summit and back, initially through thick rainforest, and then open country and edelweiss flowers. The Indonesian version of the famous Swiss plant, edelweiss seems to grow on every Indonesian volcano. On Mount Bromo in Java, women collect bunches for sale, and you're supposed to buy them and throw them into the crater for good luck or as an offering to appease any of the gods you may have upset. When I refused to buy, they were so shocked that anyone would risk not appeasing the gods that they whispered about me and stared daggers, until I felt I had made a grave error in judgement.

Alas for us though, on this trip the edelweiss on the mountain would remain unseen. The air was thick with haze, the mountain wrapped in clouds, and although it hadn't rained on us once during our journey through Sumbawa, the track here was too wet and dangerous. We would have to return.

We stopped at the house of a 'custodian' for Tambora National Park, a 'ranger' named Saiful Bahri. Saiful lived right next door to the 'gateway' to the mountain, the beginning of the trek, and he had set up a business of providing guides and porters for the groups that would arrive to climb the mountain. He was in the process of finishing the building of a five–roomed guesthouse and hoped that the 200th anniversary of the eruption would fill the rooms every night as the rest of the world became aware of it. The new guesthouse would join an older one, some fifteen minutes' walk further up the trail, as the only dedicated tourist accommodation places in the area so far. The Tambora Guest House is in the middle of a government coffee plantation near a tiny village called Oi Bura. In fact, the converted house was built by some Swedish people years ago as the plantation homestead. I didn't stay there, but it certainly looked comfortable enough.

We sat for the usual welcoming coffee in Saiful's *barugaq*, brought by his twelve–year–old daughter, Dinda. We talked about the mountain and studied the photos and a map of the trek he had pinned to a board. The map showed a number of stages between rest posts. Post 1 was three hours walk away. There were photographs taken at each of the posts, but annoyingly they showed me nothing except the grinning faces of tourists. They could have been taken anywhere.

"When it is dry it is possible to ride a motorbike up to post 1," Saiful told us.

"Can we try it today?" I asked. "Maybe it hasn't rained for a while." Saiful just laughed and shook his head.

"Too many fallen trees and too slippery."

On the map there was a little hand drawn sketch of a Hindu temple not far from where we were. "Can we get there?"

"No problem but not Iben's bike."

Hughen's Kawasaki trail bike was perfect. Subhan rode a 150 road–trail Suzuki that was nearly as good, and my aging Honda Tiger would have to do. We unloaded them, and Iben and Son settled in for a snooze as they stayed behind. Saiful took control of Subhan's bike, with him as pillion, and we set off under the arch marking the border into Bima province.

The first mud puddle was only a few metres away, and we quickly found this wasn't going to be an easy ride—unless you had a 150 Kawasaki trail bike; Hughen was ecstatic—this is what he had come for. The trail entered the forest with a thick understory of coffee bushes, and the mud got worse. I found, in some places, it was easier to stand on the ground and power the machine through the mud and ski through. Often the bikes were so locked into deep mud tracks that we just had to hang on, keep balance, and let the ruts guide us through. It was very hard work, particularly on steep sections where the road had been completely washed away. I stalled so often I started to curse my lack of an electric start button.

After twenty minutes or so, we were stopped by a tree that had fallen across the track, but a few metres ahead, we could see wooden buildings and the walls of the temple, so we parked there and walked in. I heard Saiful asking some women in the huts if it was all right for us to take photos of the temple, and they agreed without problems. A large number of tabby cats and kittens stared at us with yellow eyes from a veranda.

I was expecting the temple to be a ruin, but while old, it was beautifully maintained, adorned with a number of new statues, and clearly open for business. Balinese temples are called *pura* and this type, usually found on the sides of volcanoes, is a *pura kahyangan jagad* (temple of the celestial universe). Mountains like Tambora are considered the sacred realm of the gods. The temple's classic design had a walled outer zone, an entrance gate, and several pavilions in a central area for drums and gamelan players, and a meeting place. In the holy central zone we saw a multi–roofed pagoda, a towering lotus throne called a *padmasan* where the highest of the gods, named Acintya, dwells, and next to that a chanting platform guarded by carved concrete dragons

"This temple is very remote. How long has it been here?" I asked Saiful.

"A very long time. Balinese pilgrims come here to pray."

"So those ladies back there—they are working on the temple?"

"Yes, they are Balinese; their husbands are here too."

Rainforest surrounded the pura and I could see it was a constant battle to keep it back as small trees had been recently cleared from around the moss covered walls. Some giant trees with enormous buttress roots guarded the entrance. They were massive, perhaps fifty metres high.

"Look at those," said Hughen. "How old do you reckon they'd be—300 years?"

"Can't be a day over two hundred. Everything here was dead after the eruption." But the forest had come back with an astounding vengeance. The first naturalist to visit the mountain after the eruption actually came quite early. Heinrich Zollinger, a Swiss botanist, arrived in 1847 and climbed to the summit, recording plant and bird species as he went. Already by then, a *Casuarina* forest was growing well at the 2,200–metre level, and a number of different trees were growing on the lower slopes. The vegetation was re–establishing itself; large areas of grasslands were giving way to forests, but the ash was still "knee–deep" in parts of the lower farmlands, and the once–fertile coast of Saleh Bay was still a barren wasteland.

By the time people started to come back to settle the area, about 1907, there was a dense rainforest covering about eighty thousand hectares on the north and western slopes. Reports of 'huge, majestic forest giants' on the lower slopes and a 'montane' forest above about 1100 metres were filtering through. In 1896, someone counted fifty–six species of birds. Twelve new species were found by a survey team in 1981, and these days the count is over ninety species, some of which are hunted by the locals for the cage bird trade or for food. Few wildlife surveys make it here, so there might be others yet to be discovered. In 2013, we were excited to learn that the owl we could hear nightly, in the forests around the hill in Lombok where we lived, had just been described by an American ornithologist as a new species—the Rinjani Scops Owl. Who knew what else was out there, particularly in remote areas like Tambora?

As we left the temple, we met several coffee farmers who had come out of the forest and were now sitting on the veranda.

"Excellent road," I said to them, as we prepared to get back on the bikes.

"Ha," replied one. "You're just a learner," I took this to mean that the roads were much worse elsewhere.

On the way back to Pancasila, which was easier because gravity could do much of the work on the hills, Saiful pointed out a walking trail disappearing into the jungle.

"To the summit," he said.

So near and yet so far! The trail was calling me, but today it would have to be ignored. By the time we arrived back at Saiful's house, thick mud covered us, and he allowed us to wash some of it off with his precious tank water as we prepared to leave—after another coffee.

Saiful brought out a large book, which was the register he keeps of people who scale the mountain. There weren't that many names in it.

"Next year there will be many," said Saiful hopefully. "You must write and get us publicity. Everyone must know about Tambora and come here."

Hughen asked him about coffee. People had started living in the region again after the eruption in 1907, and in the 1930s, the Dutch government had established a coffee plantation here. Was Saiful also a farmer?

Saiful said that no, he didn't farm, but he traded a bit. The conversation continued for a while until we asked about *coffee luwak*. Is it made here, where does it come from? He disappeared into his house and returned bringing a white sack, which was about half full of green beans.

Coffee luwak has gained enormous fame as one of the most expensive coffees in the world. Its special method of production is unusual to say the least as the beans are harvested from the droppings of an animal called a luwak, a type of native civet cat, and then roasted and ground up. In our collective imaginations, luwaks lived in the forest and came into coffee plantations, ate their fill, pooped, and then returned home. Saiful's bag of beans when new weighed 15 kilograms. That is a lot of pooping!

"Where does this come from?" I asked.

"Not here, I buy this to sell to the tourists."

I sniffed the beans. Business was not good—he'd clearly had the beans for several years, as they smelled mouldy and old.

I met a luwak once. It was kept as a pet and lived not far from my home. It was a beautiful soft furred little animal that climbed on my shoulder and licked in my ear with a long rough tongue. Sadly, it didn't last long as a pet and died, like most wild animals 'rescued' from the forest.

We spent a few minutes photographing each other under the Tambora entry gate. Beside the gate was a metal information plaque written in English and one of the juicy pieces of information it dispelled was: "Napoleon Bonaparte's defeat at Waterloo in Belgium, June 18, 1815 was the impact of Tambora ash."

Several things are wrong with this often–mentioned statement in stories about Tambora. The Battle of Waterloo was only two months after the eruption, and the climatic effects of it during the *Year Without Summer* had started in late 1815 in Europe with a mild winter and then a frigid summer in 1816. By this time Napoleon was already in exile. His armies had certainly suffered through earlier severe winters—for example in 1812 during his retreat from Moscow, but this could not have had anything to do with Tambora. "The air itself," wrote a French colonel in 1812, "was thick with tiny icicles, which sparkled in the sun but cut one's face drawing blood."

All too soon, it was time to leave Pancasila—unfortunately not to climb the mountain, but to get back on the bikes and head southeast. Hughen and I were keen to stay somewhere where we could have a beer, and even Iben whose birthday was the next day was thirsty; he had become resigned to not being on Tambora's summit because of the weather and a beverage or two would be a little consolation for his special day. So we headed to the southern part of Dompu Regency, where a burgeoning tourist industry catering for surfers was blossoming—Hu'u and Lacky Beach, some four hours ride away.

Down on the coastal flats beneath Tambora, I paused to look at the walls of a gravel 'borrow–pit' the road makers were using to get their gravel. The top soil was full of plant roots and brown with humus but below that, the ash layer was obvious. It was at least two metres thick and was full of grey popcorn sized pebbles and walnut sized rocks. There were also many larger rocks, the size of beach balls, embedded in the stratum. It was a sobering thought to think they were volcanic "bombs" which had been thrown there more than twenty–five kilometres from the crater.

Chapter 7.

Death, Desolation And Disease

As we rode away from Tambora's coast and up onto the plains and rolling hills of Dompu, I reflected on what the countryside must have looked like in the weeks after the eruption. Outsiders did not know the full extent of the devastation on and around Sumbawa for several months, and the first ship to arrive was the *Benares* on the 19th April. The crew had heard the eruption from Makassar on Sulawesi, about three hundred and fifty kilometres northwest on the fifth of April, and they sailed quickly to the southeast to discover what had happened. The *Benares* stayed several days then left Bima on the twenty third of April and approached Tambora to within about ten kilometres. The captain reported the entire mountain was still smoking, particularly along several massive lava flows they could see which had reached the sea.

The second vessel to visit the area was the *Dispatch*. In the confusion, and with landmarks obliterated or covered in ash, they arrived in Sanggar by mistake on the 22nd April when looking for Bima. One of the officers went ashore, with difficulty, by a small boat and managed to meet the sultan. He didn't record the emotions the man must have been going through but wrote:

> "… the whole of his [the sultan's] country was entirely desolate, and the crops destroyed… a considerable distance from the shore being completely filled up with pumice stones, ashes, and logs of timber, the houses appeared beaten down and covered with ashes."

Reports of famine came trickling into Batavia over the following months: in August, six months after the eruption, Raffles finally responded and sent the *Benares* back, laden with rice as a form of disaster aid. Today, it seemed like a token effort, and late at that, but the fact that he sent anything at all was an indication of his humanity because in his day welfare in Asia like this was almost unknown. Sadly a few hundred tons of rice may have fed the population for no more than a week or two.

Raffles had little information to go on, of course, so he demanded full reports from his officers. Lieutenant Owen Phillips was diligent:

> "… I passed through nearly the whole of Dompo and a considerable part of Bima. The extreme misery to which the inhabitants have been reduced is shocking to behold. There were on the roadside the remains of several corpses, and the marks of where many others had been interred: the villages almost entirely deserted, and the houses fallen down, the surviving inhabitants having dispersed in search of food…

> 'Since the eruption, a violent diarrhoea has prevailed in Bima, Dompo and Sang'ir, which has carried off a great number of people.

It is supposed by the natives to have been caused by drinking water which has been impregnated with ashes; and horses have also died, in great numbers...

'The Rajah of Sang'ir came to wait on me at Dompo... The suffering of the people there appears, from his account, to be still greater than Dompo. The famine has been so severe that even one of his daughters died from hunger...

'A messenger, who returned yesterday from Sambawa (sic), relates that the fall of ashes has been heavier at Sambawa than on this side of the gulf, and that an immense number of people have been starved: they are now parting with their horses and buffaloes for a half or quarter rupee's worth of rice or corn..."

Riding through thousands of hectares of rich farmland, at its best in the February wet season, producing corn, rice, fruits, and vegetables in awesome amounts, it was hard to imagine what it would be like with a heavy layer of grey ash flattening everything into the mud. In a time when transport and communication was slow, the despair survivors would have experienced must have been excruciating, knowing that there was no one, anywhere, who could really help. All ground cover had been buried under tens of centimetres of grey ash, and taller plants carried sticky loads on all their leaves, starving them of sunlight. Lucky survivors were eating the hearts of palm trees they could cut down, but their houses had collapsed under the weight of ash on their roofs. Perhaps they had made rudimentary shelters against the weather and spent their days hunting for food and clean water, doubled over in pain from diarrhoea and slowly starving.

Today villages seem evenly spread, but often, in the Indonesian way, they are stretched along the roads with farmland behind, so they seem bigger than they really are as you pass through them.

Sumbawa has a total population of about 1.4 million people. They mostly live in Bima and Sumbawa regencies, and the whole of the Dompu Regency has less than two hundred and fifty thousand people living in it today. In the early eighteen hundreds, Sumbawa's total population was probably about one hundred and fifty thousand people, but we will never know how many people the eruption actually killed. Lieutenant Phillips was the first to make an estimate:

> 'Of the whole villages of Tomboro, Tempo, containing about forty inhabitants, is the only one remaining. In Pekate, no vestige of a house is left: twenty– six of the people, who were at Sumbawa at the time, are the whole of the population who have escaped. From the most particular enquiries I have been able to make, there were certainly not fewer than twelve thousand individuals in Tomboro and Pekate at the time of the eruption, of whom only five or six survive. The trees and herbage of every description, along the whole of the north and west sides of the peninsula, have been completely destroyed, with the exception of a high point of land near where the village of Tomboro stood...'

Phillip's estimate of twelve thousand is an intelligent guess, but the low numbers of survivors in the area around Tambora make any mortality estimate of upwards of 99 per cent a sobering thought. The village of Tambora, the people, and their entire culture and language (which were distinct from both Bimanese and Sumbawan) were wiped from the face of the earth.

Estimates of the number of slower, lingering deaths through disease or starvation in Sumbawa over the next few months suggested Tambora may have taken out a third of the total population of the island, perhaps fifty thousand people, but no census of the island either before or after the eruption can verify the numbers. However, there would certainly not have been a person on the island left unaffected as every family must have suffered deaths or severe hardship, and enormous numbers of people had to move from their now–infertile ancestral homes to become refugees in their own land. The effects further afield were also appalling. In Lombok, there may have been as many as about forty–four thousand deaths (a quarter of the population) and in Bali, up to twenty– five thousand people may have died from famine and disease. There were also reports of deaths coming from Banyuwangi in East Java where the roofs of many houses collapsed under the weight of ash and food production was severely curtailed. Further west, in West Java farmers were able to shake off the layers of ash from individual plants to maintain food production, but in Makassar, three centimetres of ash had destroyed the crops, killing plants, fish, and birds. In total, about one hundred and twenty–five thousand people are thought to have died as a direct result of the eruption, making it the deadliest eruption in recorded history.

Two hundred years is a long time, but I still hoped something so dramatic would be collectively 'remembered,' and everywhere I went in Sumbawa, I asked people if they'd heard stories passed down in their families of their ancestors' survival, but no one knew any. I was saddened when people claimed that their communities were too far from the mountain as it seemed not only that the stories have been lost, but so too had the understanding of just how big the eruption was. Life had returned to normal, and people were complacent about living on the slopes of the most devastating volcano of modern times. I shouldn't have been surprised—I built a house in Lombok near Mount Rinjani and put a lot of effort into making sure it would not collapse on my children if we had a major earthquake, but some of my neighbours have a more it–couldn't–happen–here mentality and think I wasted my money. I hope our houses are never tested.

The survivors in Sumbawa would have experienced incredibly harsh conditions for many years after the eruptions. In 1847, when Zollinger arrived, ash still covered the western end of the island and once–fertile land, including rice paddies, remained unplanted, and the villages were still abandoned. Some people had moved into the interior to start new communities, and some desperate people had sold themselves or their children into slavery, hoping for a better life without their freedom. Resettlement was slow and deliberate, and sometimes forced. For example, Sumbawa Besar, now the biggest city in western Sumbawa, was re–established by the Sultan of Sumbawa using slave labour he'd procured in southern Sulawesi.

The sun settled into the haze in the east as we passed through Dompu, and it was dark by the time we were on the road to Hu'u. People were eating their evening meals and getting on with their daily lives. I felt concerned that Tambora's history was not being taught in their local schools. They followed an Indonesian central curriculum, which had little emphasis on local history and, as a result, there seemed to be little knowledge of or reverence for the island's importance in the history of the world. I wondered, as we descended to the southern coast, if this would change with the coming bicentennial. Perhaps the whole world was about to learn some history. After all, the mountain had not been content with local influence only. The eruption was so large and violent that its effects were felt worldwide for several years.

Chapter 8.

Hu'u And The Geezers

The town of Hu'u and Lakey Beach won the Best Tourism Destination, 2013, at the Tourism Extravaganza Night in Lombok, but on arrival, in the dark on a moonless night, it was hard to see why. There were no street lights because of a power failure nor was there any indication of any real settlement. We could initially see no shops or other buildings, but Iben led us into the grounds of a hotel, and we could see why. The 'resorts' are close to the beach, as you might expect, but their blocks are long and skinny, and each has a hundred metres or so of drive way to negotiate from the road.

The hotel we had chosen was a series of double bungalows in lines down each side of the property, with a bar and restaurant in the middle at the far end, facing the beach. We could hear the surf, but the night was so dark that we ventured no further than the front fence because there seemed little point—we could explore in the morning. There were a number of Indonesian guests among the rooms, but we saw no foreigners at all until, predictably, we went into the bar.

The bar owner, an Aussie named Mick, was laid up on a platform on the side with his knee wrapped in ice after a surfing accident that afternoon. Half a dozen guys were sitting around a table, all with laptop computers or smartphones. No one was talking. I could see a couple of screens showing surfing videos—I guessed that was what surfers do when it's too dark to surf. I asked Mick if this was normal. "Yeah," he replied. "It's more like running an internet cafe than a bar. They're Pommies, but they're okay. Just here to surf."

Mick was one of those Aussie expats who had married locally, and his bar, which he leased off the Chinese hotel owners, appeared to be a marginal business indeed. Mick said he still had to return home on occasion to make money: he would leave his wife and son behind to manage the bar, return to Sydney or Canberra to do some bricklaying ("Canberra pays better" he said), and then hurry back to his family and the surf.

I ordered a couple of bottles of Bintang beer, which duly arrived semi–cold as Mick had used all the ice on his knee.

"The freezer is busted." Mick sighed. "If you're in for a session, I can send someone up the road to buy some more."

"Perhaps one or two," I suggested tentatively with a feeling that I was putting him to great trouble, but he gave a bundle of cash to one of his staff who duly set off on his motorbike to return a few minutes later with five bottles of ice cold beer. By nine pm, the surfers were packing up to go to bed, and Hughen, Iben, and I sat on the veranda listening to the surf and looking at the rotting furniture, the faded and torn sign that said "H PPY E YE R," which nobody had bothered to take down, and the thick layer of dust and grime that lay over all the surfaces.

One young bloke came out on his way back to his room. "Good night geezers," he said as he passed.

"*Geezers*! Bloody cheek! Are we there already?" I asked his retreating back as he slouched away, but got no reply.

"We're not as young as we used to be," observed Hughen. "Anyway, he was looking at you, not me."

We toasted Iben's 39th birthday. Nobody called him a geezer, but I did overhear someone say his dreadlocks were 'rad'. Then, just to prove we were still young and had stamina, we out–partied all the young punk surfers, and we were the last to leave, staggering off to bed about nine–thirty.

The next morning proved an eye opener in more ways than one. Iben and I went down to the beach early and bought coffee from a little *warung* on the sand run by a toothless old woman who had four broken plastic chairs around a tiny fire place. A concrete tower stood watch over the surf, and we climbed it to survey the beach.

At low tide, the surf was several hundred metres away, but a few surfers were out on their boards already. Another tower sitting in the water on a reef stood as testament to surfing photography and the judging of 'world class' Lakey Beach surf competitions, which should be well known to all surfers. This place was the real deal, but in February the surf was flat. Mick had complained that for two weeks in January there had been no surf at all, and the surfers who had turned up had nearly died of boredom. "Why couldn't they watch the surf on YouTube like your current guests?" I had asked quietly but got no response.

There was a tsunami around these parts in August 1977 following a large earthquake to the south. Unfortunately, the precursor of a tsunami is the withdrawal of much of the water along the coast, and children and adults were tempted down to see the strange sight and pick up stranded fish. Swept away to their deaths, more than thirty people in Sumbawa, and another twenty–five in Lombok died from the effects of the tsunami. Hopefully these days, especially after extended TV coverage of the huge tsunami of 2004 in Aceh, people are more educated about the danger of sudden sea level drops, and they head for the hills rather than the beach.

Iben was prepared to let us sit out the day here and relax but was relieved to hear that I really wanted to move on to Bima. If we left early, we could get to the museum before it closed and see the town. I don't think any of us were impressed by what we had seen so far.

When the others emerged, Hughen and I went to see about the surfers' breakfast, which was included with the room, whilst Iben, Subhan, and Son wisely opted for Indo-nesian street food and wandered further down the beach.

The surfers shared a large table outside the breakfast kitchen to feast on the banana pancakes that all westerners eat wherever they go, apparently, as if it is what they normally have at home. Only one man was there when we arrived. He was a Californian.

"Aussies? Yeah I am going to Australia to do the fuckin' twelve– month working visa thing it'll be fuckin' awesome flying straight to Perth from fuckin' Lombok fuckin' *easy as* heard there's some fuckin' sick surf there too my buddy says he was in the fuckin' line up and some of these guys'd just fuckin' drop outta the line to go into these fuckin' shark cages to see the fuckin' sharks in the same fuckin' waves man, fuckin' awesome yeah! A fuckin' sick booster eh!"

Hughen and I looked at each other. We were saved when two young blokes and a girl from Dorset turned up and joined the conversation.

"Banana pancakes," they called to the old lady serving breakfast. "We arrived last night. Sick place, hey? We got to Bima and took a taxi straight here—700,000 rupiah! Airport prices... but it was, like, crazy there, and it only took two hours. Coffee... yes? How are you geezers travelling?"

"Who, us? Err, we're on motorbikes, from Lombok."

"Sick! You hear that Bern. Riding a bike through Sumbawa would be sick."

A giant Aussie with short cropped hair and the thickest blonde beard I have ever seen sat down at the table. His piercing light blue eyes surveyed us all.

"Is your name Erik?" I asked him.

"No, Barry," he replied. "Why?"

"I can guess your ancestry easy enough." He made no reply and turned his Viking gaze to the Dorset guys.

"G'day, you guys were in Bali, yeah? We got some sick rides there, hey?"

"Yes," said the one who wasn't Bern. "You in that last big swell that came through?"

"Sure was. There were some seriously sick barrels. Real grunty groundswell, like 23 seconds, hey! I got into this cracker barrel, geez, sick or what? I was frothin'. Hey, you've only been riding 12 months haven't you? Standing up real well. Natural. Some people are still on their knees. Any surf in Dorset?"

Another Australian arrived and told us he ran a mobile coffee machine business from his bicycle in Fremantle. He'd been around Sumbawa looking for green *Arabica* beans he could take back home and seemed to be the only surfer in the crowd who made any sense.

I told him of the *kopi luwak* beans we'd seen the day before. "Nah, wouldn't touch them," he said immediately.

"I read an article about coffee luwak. In the beginning it was all right, they used to collect the beans from turds on the ground, and the luwak were free to choose the best fruit. Nowadays, they have them in small cages like chickens and force–feed them any rubbish fruit they have, and then just scoop the shit up. It's really bad."

"I want to know," said Viking, "who the sick bastard is who found out if you drink coffee that had come out of some animal's shit it would, like, taste good."

"That cafe has coffee luwak,' California was saying. "Fuckin' awesome food right next door sick homemade fuckin' tortillas fuckin' awesome."

"I hate being white," said Dorset girl. "You guys are getting sick tans. "Fuckin' ay!"

"It's okay. Indonesians like white skin. They don't want to be brown. Pass the honey."

"Oh, is that honey? I didn't know what it was. Sick."

Hughen and I had gone quiet. We had nothing to add to this conversation, and I was secretly trying to write notes of what these guys were saying. Iben passed by and said he had finished breakfast. When did we want to move on?

"Wow, sick dreads," Dorset girl whispered.

"Ready now," I replied. I looked at Hughen. "Well, you old geezer, about time you and I got our sorry asses back into the saddle and, like, boosted the road again. Come on, it's gonna be sick."

"Yeah, right on mate. Sick breakfast, hey?"

"See youse blokes later," I drawled. "And remember to stay loose in the saddle and mind your old world charm and dignity..."

"What did he say?" Dorset girl whispered again.

We left Hu'u aware that we'd witnessed a culture which was as understandable to 'old geezers' like us as the latest smartphone. We had had glimpses through a little window into a world from a different dimension, and I reckon it is frothin' sick the way the world moves, like, in mysterious ways, hey.

Back on the bikes, we had a chance to see the countryside we'd passed through in the dark the night before. There were areas of rice paddies and other farms, but also tree plantations as the countryside started to get hilly. Teak trees were common, notable because they were heavily in flower and looking so much more pleasant than in the dry season when they shed most of their leaves. Teak comes originally from the forest of Burma and northern Thailand, but it has been in Indonesia for so many centuries that its origin is forgotten by zealous people keen to save ancient wild teak trees in some of the country's forest, despite them actually being a feral weed species.

A few villages are strung out along the road. I knew that this southern part of the island had been less affected by Tambora's eruption than the plains near Dompu and Bima, but there had been an ash fall tens of centimetres thick. At the time, the area was sparsely populated, so few problems arose, and the farmers were now beneficiaries of the volcanic nutrients. Settlement patterns in the modern world react to different forces, but two hundred years ago, some of the interior villages had been settled because Tambora's effects had been worse along the coast. People had moved inland whilst ash still buried the flat coastal areas. Ash is eventually good for soil fertility, but this takes a few years, and crops continued to fail. In hilly areas, rainfall washed the ash away more easily and the soils were ready for planting earlier.

Riding through some low hills, I noticed a number of blue tarpaulins that I thought might mark mine diggings among the trees on the hillside. Blue tarps are a sign of illegal mining operations in the south of Lombok; sure enough, down by a river, hundreds of drums connected to small petrol engines were slowly turning, separating gold from the soil, and I stopped to have a look. The gold fever that has swept the Sekotong area of Lombok over the last few years has reportedly killed hundreds of men through cave–ins of their unsupported tunnels, mercury poisoning, and other accidents. The authorities raid every now and then and clear away the unclaimed motorbikes left there by miners who never returned, but there seems to be little else they can do, or have the will to do, about them. Nobody really has any idea how many people are involved, but there are even stories of enterprising Mataram residents having a truckload of dirt and rocks from Sekotong delivered to their backyards in town, so they can go through it and extract the gold at their leisure, unfortunately, at the same time, delivering mercury into the suburbs where thousands of other people live.

Although here it was clearly a much smaller operation, I wondered whether Sumbawa was having the same problems and asked the man who was attending the drums. He shrugged, either not knowing or not understanding my questions but giving me an odd look that left me with the feeling that he was just not willing to discuss the subject. I hid my suspicions and wished him well, and having fallen well behind the others, hurried to catch up with them on the road to Bima.

Iben has a brother–in–law living in a village between Dompu and Bima, and we stopped there for a *bakso* lunch. Hughen and I were an immediate big hit with the village children. They flocked to get a glimpse of us, and a crowd gathered outside. In the end, we had to pose for a series of photographs with groups of kids, hold babies, and sign a few autographs, but thankfully, Iben's brother–in–law chased the crowd away when the food was ready.

Bakso is a national favourite found right across Indonesia. It is basically meat ball soup, using the cheapest cuts of meat. It is most often served with noodles, and the recipe varies from place to place. Here, near Bima, it also has a hardboiled egg in it, wrapped in a jacket of the same meat as the meat ball. It was hot, cooked to perfection, and the first of many Hughen came to enjoy in Indonesia—by the time he left he was in danger of becoming an addict.

Subhan lives about a twenty–minute ride outside of Bima, and he'd invited us to stay with him overnight. His house is set behind some paddy fields next to a community open–air volleyball court. A small flock of ducks waddled around his back yard where a squash known as *labu Siam* in Indonesia (Siamese gourd), grew in profusion on vines supported by a metal frame. It is a large house, with high ceilings and tiled floors, and he was living alone, although not by choice. He revealed to us that he had a wife who, three months before, had had a baby boy in Jakarta, but he wasn't allowed to travel by plane until he was six months old and by bus it was too far. So Subhan, who couldn't afford to fly to Jakarta, hadn't yet met his son and he was waiting anxiously for his wife's return.

We left our gear in the house and once again climbed on the bikes to head to Bima. I was keen to get to the Bima museum and hoped it wouldn't be closed on a Saturday afternoon. The road led us around the bay where large areas of low dykes are built on the tidal floodplains. These were salt farms. The owners flood them and then evaporate the water, and it is said that they can harvest up to two tonnes of salt per hectare during the four–month season from June.

Further around, machines churning the water marked some fish or prawn farms. Small stilted buildings overlooked them, which I assumed were for night guards or respite from the sun for day workers.

We passed a large Balinese temple on the edge of Bima and entered the city. Built around the bay, from first sight Bima seemed a delightful seaside town; with large numbers of horse drawn carts, they call *Ben Hurs* (after the movie's chariots). We were quickly embroiled in the traffic and had to jostle to keep up with Iben as we worked our way into the centre.

The town square, called the *alun–alun*, in the centre of town, stretched out in front of the *kraton*, the sultan's palace. The kraton had a gatehouse with an elaborate wooden roof and big metal gates. They were open and, as there was no security guard, we just rode on in and parked in front of a broad white stone stair case leading up to the palace veranda.

A four year old jockey of Sumbawa.

The child jockeys of Sumbawa ride small stallions

By age seven the jockeys are too big for the horses and retire.

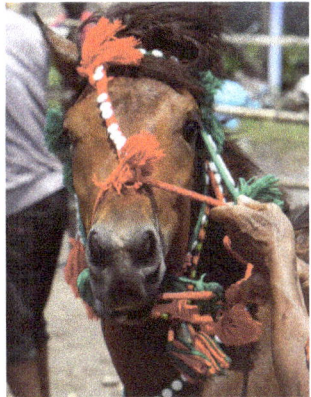

The small Sumbawa horses possibly descend from South African stock brought here during the Dutch era.

Many children: Bungin Island claims to be the most densely populated island in the world.

Village soccer match, Pancasila.

The extraordinary fertility of the volcanic land produces bumper crops such as this garlic.

Roadside mechanic in Sumbawa.

The current sultan of Sumbawa Besar still uses this Dutch-built
kraton (palace).

The Istana Dalam Loka is the old Sultan's Palace in Sumbawa Besar.

Throughout Indonesia motor scooters are essential transportation.

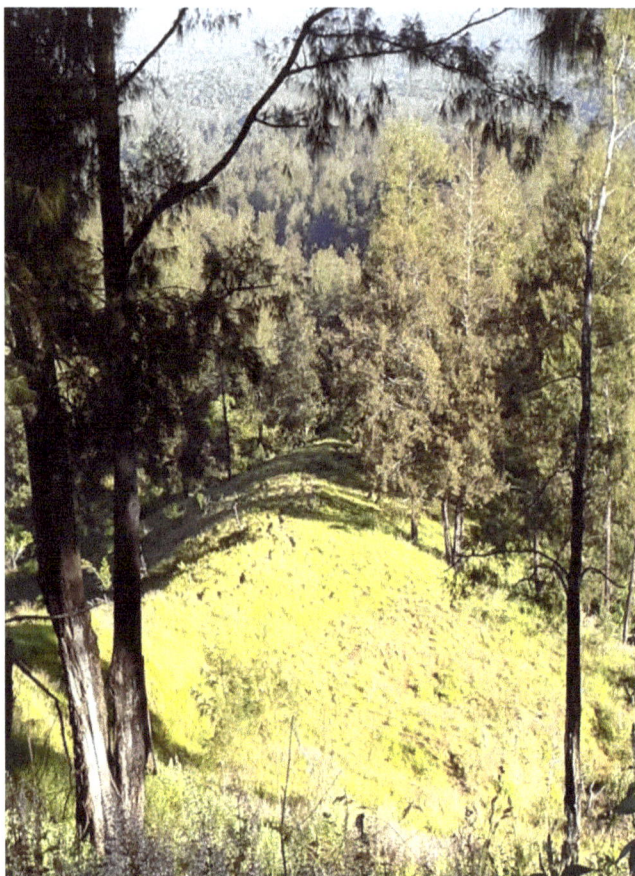

Casuarina trees were some of the first to recolonise the upper
slopes of Tambora after the eruption.

Tambora in February.

Nearly 25 km from the summit the fallout from the eruption is still evident.

Tambora. The sound of rocks falling from the cliffs is continuous.

Tambora's crater is 7km in diameter, 21 km in circumference and
800m deep.

Thick forests on the slopes of Tambora.

The walk up Tambora is divided into five rest posts.

Tambora is still active. Plumes of gas rise from the crater regularly.

Sumbawan Houses

Sumbawan Houses

Tambora.

Bungin Island goats are famous throughout
Indonesia for their meagre diet.

There's a gold rush going on in
the hills of Sumbawa and the
tumblers run continuously.

Bungin Island, dwarfed by Lombok's Mt Rinjani.

In Sumbawa travellers are always a big hit in the villagers.

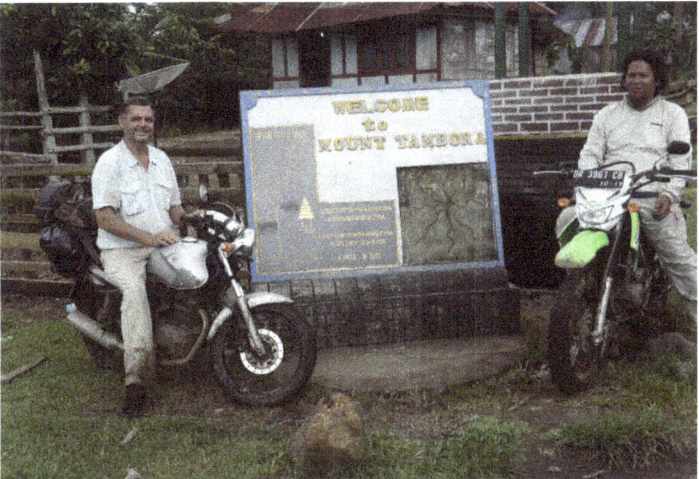

The author with Poax Iben at the gateway to the mountain at Pancasila.

Sri Sultan Bima
Muhammad Salahuddin
Ibnu Sultan Ibrahim
(1888-1951), the 16th
Sultan of Bima and
Ibu Maryam's father.

The princess, Ibu Siti Maryam, Paux Iben,
and the author with the Bo Saugaji Kai.

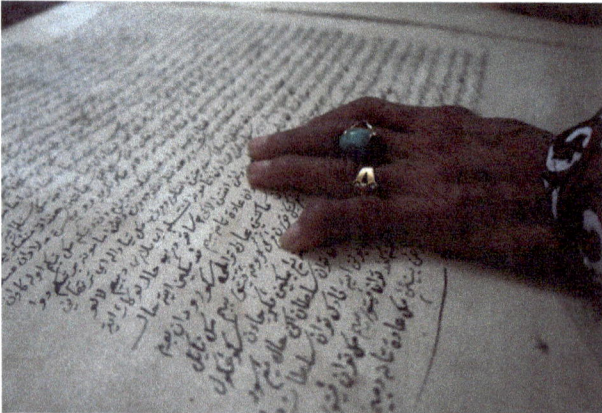

The Bo Saugaji Kai, 'The Book of the Kingdom' is a 400 year
history written by the Sultans of Bima.

Chapter 9.

Bima And The Anti–Sultan

In Bima the *kraton* is no longer the sultan's home, although he still uses it for ceremonial or festive occasions. Most of the time the *kraton* is kept as a museum, which is usually open to the public. Unfortunately, when we arrived the doors were closed because the sultan had died only a few weeks before, and the kraton was still under the official forty–day period of mourning. However, the open gate had been welcoming, and no one took any notice of our arrival as we rode through them. Several young couples sat together in the shade of some giant trees, giggling like young couples everywhere and large numbers of deer roamed freely around the grounds.

Built in 1927, the kraton is a large two–story house. Huge verandas, supported by thick pillars, wrap its sides. Some faded black and white photos hang in simple frames on their walls, so we wandered up the stairs to look closer.

The photos mostly showed groups of people at ceremonial occasions of the past or traditional musical instruments.

On an impulse, I tried the front door, and the rattle of the handle quickly brought an old man from inside.

"Good morning, *Bapak*. We know you are closed. Do you think we can come in and have a look? We have come a long way." And so, as simply as that, we were invited into the kraton museum. Its entry hall is large with a steep wooden staircase leading upstairs on one side and hallways heading off both left and right to give access to the lower rooms. These days the downstairs rooms are mostly empty except for a few dusty display cases showing some old clothing, a few porcelain pots, two small, plain sedan chairs, a couple of old rifles, and some chain–mail, but little else. Oddly, there were two huge vases of beautiful fresh–cut flowers standing on either side of the staircase, despite the museum being closed.

We were led upstairs. This is where the recent sultans had lived with their families. Still furnished in a 1930s era decor, the bedrooms have wardrobes and chests of drawers from Europe, carved Chinese armchairs, and four–poster beds. The rooms aren't large, and water marks on the ceilings and faded peeling paint belie the fact that this was a royal palace. The last sultan, who was the seventeenth of his lineage, had moved to a house a few hundred metres away, and it seems few funds have been spent on maintenance since then, although the old man who was our guide did mention some restoration in 1973.

Looking out the windows from the upstairs corridors, I could see, across an open park (the *alung*), a flat–roofed vinyl shade tent with rows of white plastic chairs on the road in front of a house where the latest sultan had actually lived. This was where mourners could come and join in the daily prayers to farewell the old sultan.

The palace was slowly succumbing to neglect. I passed the toilets and bathrooms and entered what would have been a servants' area. It was without a ceiling, and I was interested to see the roof joists and the wooden skeleton of the building, but the old man called me back immediately because the floor wasn't safe to walk on. I could imagine his embarrassment if I'd suddenly plunged through the boards into the kitchens below on a day he was supposed to keep the museum locked up.

There was an ancient handwritten Koran open on a chest of drawers in the sultan's bedroom, and we could picture him standing there reading it. Iben posed in front of it for a photo, pretending to read. In the hall were plastic mannequins wearing old clothes. I stood between two and posed for my own photo, and the old man took a *topi* off the head of the mannequin beside me and placed it on mine. "Spot the dummy," I said.

There was very little of any real value in the museum, and with the low security we'd witnessed, we could understand why. According to our guide, the sultan's family now keeps valuable items under lock and key elsewhere.

Iben had told me weeks earlier that we might have been able to meet the sultan, who had been a keen amateur historian himself, so his death was untimely in terms of our visit. After the old man ushered us outside, we sat on the front veranda to discuss what to do next. A short stocky man proudly growing three or four long black hairs from a mole on his face joined us. Iben knew him and introduced him to us as the "Assistant Sultan," which I correctly took to mean 'assistant to the sultan'. He is a pleasant man, then in his mid–fifties, and Iben apparently knew him quite well. They talked for a while, and Iben announced that we would be able to meet with the "anti–sultan" that afternoon. I didn't know what an anti–sultan was but figured that maybe he was a stand-in before the new sultan was proclaimed. The future Sultan (the eighteenth) was still a student in Jakarta, so perhaps there'd be a year or two of rule by the 'anti–sultan' whilst he was still studying. Curious, I asked Iben if this was what was happening, but the Assistant Sultan distracted him, and I let it slide because the mystery would clear itself up when we made our visit and I was distracted myself: the man's mole hairs waved about as he spoke like tiny semaphores and when he laughed they whipped back on themselves like they had a life of their own. Anyway, our plans changed again when we were told that the anti–sultan was in prayers with the mourners and not available. He would, however, be happy to meet with us the next morning.

After we'd finished at the museum, we rode up the hill named *Dana Taraha* which overlooks Bima. This is where the seventeen deceased Sultans are buried. Sultan Abdul Kahir, the first sultan, who reigned from 1630 until his death in 1640, had a simple hemispherical concrete bunker grave, which looked so much younger than 374 years; I suspect it had been rebuilt. Iben entered it briefly to pray.

Metal bars caged the grave of sultan number 4, one had a wooden shelter with a shingle roof, but the others were simple constructions marking a patch of earth. The graves were labeled with laminated, faded paper signs, which announced the names of their occupants and dates of their burial. Buried there too was the last sultan, the seventeenth. He had a blue tarpaulin above him for shade, and the clay of his grave was already hardening. There were a few flowers around but no real indication of what the grave will look like when it is a permanent construction. The Bimanese are

Muslims, of course, and unlike the local Chinese who maintain massive mausoleums to their ancestors, most Muslim graves remain simple affairs. It appeared that even the sultans followed this custom.

From the hill, we headed to the waterfront for coffee. Bima sits beside an enormous, picturesque, sheltered inlet several kilometres across. A small volcano named Mount Orambuha stands on the far side of the bay from Bima and it stops any view from there of Tambora, only 65 kilometres away as the crow flies. Unfortunately there was so much haze that day we could hardly even see Orambuha.

As it was *malam minggu*—the Saturday 'date' night—weekend stallholders were setting up sitting places around the water where people could meet with their friends, drink coffee, and eat noodles. Some of the stalls were fenced metal and concrete constructions with roofs, the size and shape of the pens you see at Australian country fairs built to hold competition livestock. They were stretched right around the bay, and in a strict Muslim city, such as Bima, they may well be major venues for the high points of Friday and Saturday night entertainment.

We enjoyed hot steamy Sumbawan coffee and watched the world pass us by for an hour before heading back to Subhan's house for the night. On the way, Hughen and I bought some takeaway beer from a local *warung,* and, having an aversion to warm beer, we also picked up a bag of ice to take with us as Subhan didn't own a fridge.

The next morning we were getting ready to leave to meet the anti–sultan. Hughen asked Iben if he would need to wear long trousers and boots rather than his sandals. Iben nodded.

"Old ladies, you see. More respect," he said. I had visions of the royal court—the anti–sultan sitting on his throne, old ladies in waiting attending to his needs, glancing with horror at Hughen's hairy knees.

"Gotta have respect," I added smugly.

We loaded up the bikes because after our audience with royalty the plan was to ride the full length of the island back to Taliwang.

"I wonder how old she is," mused Hughen.

"Who?" I asked.

"The aunt," he replied. "She must be quite old if her father died in 1951.

"Whose aunt?"

"The sultan's aunt, the woman we're about to visit."

"What? Ah I see..." In a flash, it was all suddenly clear. In the same way Iben had introduced the assistant to the sultan as the 'assistant sultan' he had also described the sultan's aunt as the '*aunty sultan*'.

There is no such thing as an 'anti–sultan,' and it's quite likely always been that way. We started the bikes and set off for Bima with me feeling a bit of a dill, and Hughen mumbling something about me having cloth ears. I didn't even try to explain my misunderstanding to Iben.

We arrived at the aunt's house a little after 8.30. It is a normal, though large, suburban house on a reasonably busy street. Some of the rooms on its right side have been turned into a small museum, guarded by the obligatory old Dutch canon. In the garden and facing out to the street there was a giant political poster for a woman running for election. Her photo was over a metre high–a huge balloon head wrapped in a blue headscarf. In the corner of the poster an older woman's photo caught my attention.

Was this the aunt?

We took off our shoes on the porch, and Iben led us to the open front door. Inside a woman with heavy makeup and a peach–coloured head scarf sat next to an old lady, posing for a photograph, so we waited quietly on the side. The room clearly belonged to an old lady, and I remembered many like it owned by my own great aunts decades ago—full of aging furniture, hundreds of books and photos, doilies, and cut flowers. It had that peculiar homely smell that pervades old people's houses, of dust, mildew, lavender soap and vegetable soup. Three tennis racquets hung on one wall and there were several trophies. A row of plaques, of the type which are commonly presented at special events in Indonesia, were propped open in their boxes along one bookshelf, and vases of flowers stood among the various souvenirs and knick–knacks she had collected over the years.

Hughen recognised the woman being photographed from the poster outside—this was a candidate for the next election; not a balloon-head after all, but an ambitious determined woman with a heavily painted face. After her photographs were taken, she was ushered away to sit on chairs across the room and forgotten. From her body language, I could tell she was mightily annoyed, but by then we were being entertained by royalty, so I didn't give her another thought until she huffily said her goodbyes and stalked off a few minutes later.

Iben formally introduced me to Ibu Siti Maryam, daughter of the 16th Sultan of Bima, a *putri*, or princess. She was tiny, with the age–bent body and slow movements of the elderly. Iben bowed and touched his forehead to her hand, and Subhan, Hughen, and I both followed his lead and did the same. She seemed fragile and there was something about her that immediately made me feel protective—and I wasn't the only one as later, when she moved across the room, we almost fell over each other to be her steadying hand. But none of us could compete with Subhan. A Bimanese himself, this old lady was *his* royalty, and he clearly had great affection for her—if she needed care while we were there, then he was just the man for the job. I thought he'd probably fight me for the honour.

"Nice to meet you," she said to me in English but, although I suspected she could speak English fluently, she used very little after that. She sat on a couch beneath photos of a younger version of herself visiting Versailles and Paris, Jerusalem, and London, and she talked briefly about her travels. She had grown up in the *kraton* in Bima, and I wondered, but didn't ask, if she ever compared the opulence of Versailles with her own palace upbringing. We had visited her austere childhood bedroom upstairs in the *kraton* only yesterday, and it was a poor comparison even to the bedrooms many modern day Indonesians have in their big city houses.

Iben explained about my interest and research into Tambora and told her of my plans to write about it. In fact, he expanded on my virtues and seemed not at all shy about his use of hyperbole, while I sat quietly, slightly embarrassed, and put up with it in case this use of such flowery and complimentary language was normal protocol—after all, this was my first brush with royalty.

"...he is very famous in his country. Pak Derek has written many books, and his writing brings great prestige to the place he writes about. He is writing now about Sumbawa and Tambora and..."

The introduction had the right effect, and she was immediately open to my interviewing. I asked what she knew of the mountain and its eruption, and it quickly became clear she had a great deal of knowledge and, in fact, had the original writings of the sultan of the time about the eruption. Would I like to see them?

"*Mau*!" I said. In English, it just means *want*. As a single word, it might have appeared a little bad mannered, but in Bahasa Indonesia when said with enthusiasm, it seemed the appropriate response, my version of "yes, please". The princess rose slowly to weave her way through the numerous chairs of her sitting room. Subhan leapt to her service and helped her negotiate the path through the furniture. He would have gladly piggy backed her if she'd asked. Along the wall was a glass fronted bookcase full of old leather–bound books and one, a very large green book was clearly visible. Iben carefully took it down and carried it over. This man of letters, with several degrees in history and sociology behind him had his hands on a very precious volume indeed, and he was nearly in tears of excitement. It was the *Bo Saugaji Kai*, an almost holy book for him, written by the sultans through the ages to record special events in their domain. Iben's hands shook as he placed the book on the table and waited, squirming like a toddler waiting under the tree on Christmas morning, for Ibu Maryam to be seated once again to open it.

When she was ready, she opened the book at random to reveal incredibly neat Arabic script for page after page. A faint smell of age rose from the pages as Iben modestly admitted he could read a little Arabic. He and the princess leafed slowly through the book looking for the right era. It must be an extraordinary feeling for her to read the writings of her grandfathers over hundreds of years. I picked out a few dates in the text—1716, 1845, and other years, but the rest was unintelligible to me. Finally the Tambora page was found, and Iben struggled to translate it. He could see it mentioned the Tambora kingdom and a 'bad' sultan and they were destroyed by the eruption, but without a dictionary, he could do little more.

"There is, of course, a translation in the museum next door," said

Ibu Maryam.

She had been struggling to read the text too but blamed cataracts. She said she needed to have them operated on but was scared of the operation. I encouraged her—both my parents had had the operation in their eighties, and they could see again *seperti sulap*, like magic! Hughen's grandmother had had a cataract operation at ninety–four, and the princess seemed emboldened on hearing this.

In the background, one of her staff had been fussing with some cloth and sarongs. She called her over with them and talked for a while about their quality. They certainly were beautiful woven artworks. She surprised me by giving me one.

"Choose one for your wife," she said.

I was stunned. "Wow, the blue one you are holding, thank you, *terimah khasi banyak*." I had already taken some really nice photographs of her with the blue cloth while she was folding it. I knew that that would mean it to be even more special to The Lovely Rina, who loves woven cloth but also has an Indonesian's high regard for their aristocracy.

Then, after we had put the book away, and posed for photographs with her as no doubt many thousands of people had done before, Ibu Maryam, once again supported by the faithful and now smitten Subhan, led us next door to her museum. It was her private collection, she said, and she had several display cases of porcelain, pin boards of newspaper articles and photographs, official framed photographic portraits of several sultans, chiefly her grandfather, number fifteen and her father, number sixteen, who held such an uncanny family resemblance to each other, I had thought they were photographs of the same man. There was an article about the princess as a three–year–old dated 1930—she was born in June 1927, the same year as my father.

"My father was born a month after you in 1927," I told her. "You are also a year older than Mickey Mouse."

She laughed and asked me where I was from and, when I told her Darwin, she recalled a Bima–Darwin connection:

"Ah yes, QANTAS Airlines used to fly here from Darwin." Her memory was good. In 1938, QANTAS had flying boats routed directly from the Northern Territory of Australia via Bima, which was a refuelling depot.

On a lectern, there was a full sized replica of the *Bo Saugaji Kai*, and two published books about it, one of them a direct translation into Indonesian. Iben read some of it aloud. Quickly it became apparent that it was written as poetry, in verses. Iben's voice rang out as if he was a stage performer.

"Beautiful," Iben said several times when he'd finished. He was enraptured. The verses described how the volcano had erupted because God was angry with the Sultan of Tambora, Raja Abdul Gafur. He was apparently guilty of forcing a pious Muslim *haji* named Mustafa, a pilgrim who had just returned from Mecca, to eat dog meat before killing him without mercy. This is the stuff of folk tales, but here it was in the *Bo*! A few years later, in 1830, it was quoted by a poet from Bima in a poem:

> *Its noise reverberated loudly*
>
> *Torrents of water mixed with ash descended*
>
> *Children and mothers screamed and cried*
>
> *Believing the world had turned to ash.*

The cause was said to be the wrath of God Almighty,

At the deed of the King of Tambora,

In murdering a worthy pilgrim, spilling his blood

Rashly and thoughtlessly

(Syair Kerajaan Bima)

The eruption had destroyed both the king and his kingdom, and his legacy might be a tough one, we may never know much more about him. Most of the other sultans of the island recovered from the catastrophe over time and continued to manage the island under rule from the Dutch, after they returned and ousted the English. These days only the sultans of Sumbawa Besar and Bima are still in office.

Ibu Maryam was proud of her museum, but her cataracts were hiding the dismal nature of it from her. The glass display cases were so dirty that it was hard to see inside, and in a house full of otherwise obsequious young staff it made me angry to think they were too lazy to clean properly and were getting away with it. They weren't even watering her potted plants.

At one point she drew my attention to two cheap plastic dolls about 20 centimetres tall. They were still in the plastic box they were bought in, but now it was grimy with dust and age. Souvenir shops the world over sell similar items, but these dolls were modelling Sumbawan traditional clothing. Ibu Maryam gave a royal roll of her eyes and tut–tutted, and I nodded as if I understood, but it wasn't until afterwards that I realised that they were models of her and her husband at their wedding, decades ago.

About two dozen armchairs were placed in a circle in the room. Ibu Maryam said she often showed school children and college groups around her museum and was pleased that young people showed interest in history. We talked about life in Bima, and she asked me about living in Lombok. She said she hadn't been there for several years.

"But Ibu," I said, "we are going there today. Would you like to join us, you can sit behind me on the bike."

She laughed. "I don't like the bumps, I would fall off."

She invited us to return to Bima in September as she would be holding a *Kraton* Festival. I said I would try to come, and we took our leave, climbed back on the bikes, and rode 450 kilometres westwards to Taliwang, fare–welling Subhan near his home on the way.

Tambora was still lying there to our north, shrouded in its own February weather, unconquered, but inviting us like a siren, to mount its sides and stand aloft in its battlements.

"I'll be back," I said to the north, in a fake Austrian accent.

Chapter 10.

Suffer The World

Riding almost the full length of Sumbawa in a single day gave me more than just a sore backside. It also gave an idea of the size the initial ash cloud and the speed with which it travelled. The whole of Sumbawa Besar had been engulfed during the first day after the initial eruption on the evening of the fifth of April 1815, and ash continuously fell over the next five days. So, when the major eruption occurred on the tenth, and the skies went black for two or three more days after that, the continuous ash fall must have been prodigious and terrifying for the population.

The road follows the northern coast of Sumbawa Besar, and Tambora sits in the north for much of the way on the far side of Saleh Bay. On a clear day, we'd be aware of it all the time, but the thick haze which had dogged us for days was yet to give up. Somewhere north of us, Tambora hid behind a curtain like a guilty child who had been caught being very naughty.

Teaching some secondary students about Tambora recently, I started off with a story. Story telling is one of the most powerful teaching strategies, and the story of the girl, her lover, the monster, and a far off tropical island has always had the makings of a good lesson. The girl was eighteen–year–old Mary Godwin and her lover, soon to be husband, the poet Percy Bysshe Shelley. In 1816, they were on holiday with Lord Byron and staying in a villa on Lake Geneva in Switzerland. It was cold and wet—so cold they rarely went outside, unusual indeed in the middle of summer but, in Europe that year, there was no summer.

The guests had been reading German horror stories to each other as they sat around the fire, and on one long evening, the story goes, Lord Byron challenged his young guests to a writing competition. Who could write the best horror story? Mary said, later, she dreamed hers and wrote a story which was destined to be not only one of the most enduring of all horror stories, but the first novel of a new genre; science fiction. Her monster was Frankenstein's monster, born in 1816, the *Year Without Summer* and the stormy dark skies we imagine, or remember, from old movies beneath which the story is set, recall the reality of that year.

Young Mary Godwin married Percy to become Mary Shelley and, in 1818, published this most famous of novels, initially anonymously. No one realised then that Frankenstein and his monster and the awful weather they experience in the novel had a genesis deep within a volcano thousands of kilometres away and a truth that was as terrifying as any science fiction story.

Kids are usually hooked by a story like this and want to find out more. How can a volcano so far away in the southern hemisphere affect the weather in Europe? What else did it do? Why don't all volcanoes have this effect?

The climate anomaly actually lasted three years, and for many millions of people it wasn't a *"Year Without Summer"*. A 'year' suggests an inconvenient need for an extra jacket for a few months or the need to throw another log on the fire. Rather it was three years of suffering and misery without food and fighting diseases from which there was no defence. Wretched people across the world survived or died eating nettle leaves, moss, hedgehogs, and cats.

The chemical I have always mostly associated with volcanoes is sulphur. When I was teaching in Bandung, my students would scrape crystals of it out of fumaroles on the Javanese volcanoes we would visit on middle school science fieldtrips whist waiting for our lunch: we would cook eggs in boiling pools of water on the mountain's side. Sulphur's bright yellow colour and distinctive smell make it memorable. A common gas it forms is the poisonous sulphur dioxide, and more than 55 million tons of this were ejected with the dust from Tambora up to forty–three kilometres straight up, far enough to enter the stratosphere. The sulphur dioxide reacted with the abundant water vapour, and together they formed more than 100 million tons of sulphuric acid (H_2SO_4). The acid took the form of a fine aerosol and this was whipped around the planet rapidly by the jet streams as fast as one hundred kilometres per hour. It took two weeks to cover the tropics and only a few months to cover the whole planet, pole to pole.

The stratosphere is an important layer of our atmosphere. It is usually stable and dry, above the water found in the troposphere below, and no rain or clouds form there. It is also warmer at the bottom than it is further out, but is still colder than the troposphere, so there is little mixing between the two, and water rarely enters it. So, with no rain to clean it, there was nothing but the slow pull of gravity on the cloud to pull the acid droplets and the dust particles back down to earth. This is why it lasted several years, reflecting sunlight from the earth, cooling the surface, and bringing miserable weather to hundreds of millions of people across the globe. The planet Venus has an atmosphere that is largely sulphuric acid, and one of the reasons it is so bright in our sky is that sulphuric acid clouds reflect light very well. The result is that Venus is brighter than Mercury even though the latter is closer to the sun.

Nineteenth–century people knew little of this science, but now we know that the Earth, our most beautiful and unique planet, was veiled like a dictator lying in state, cooling as the energy that brought it life faded to blackness. But even the term 'veil' hides the horror of what it really was. It was not a soft muslin cloth delicately wrapped, but a malevolent stratospheric layer of sulphuric acid denying us our allotted share of solar radiation.

My father used to recite a little rhyme about sulphuric acid he'd learned at primary school in the 1930s, so from a young age I knew it was pretty nasty stuff:

> *Little Johnny's gone aloft,*
>
> *He'll bother us no more,*
>
> *For what he thought was H_2O*
>
> *Was H_2SO_4.*

All eruptions produce amounts of dust and sulphur dioxide that enter the atmosphere, but only some are powerful enough to shoot a very large quantity very high. The timing of Tambora's eruption was unfortunate as there had been a number of other large eruptions of volcanoes, which had also injected dust into the stratosphere in the years just prior to 1815, (Mounts Mayon in the Philippines, (1814) and Suwanosejima in Japan (1813)) so it was already carrying a load, but Tambora's contribution took it 'over the top.'

Some of the effects were aesthetic. Magnificent sunsets of yellow, orange, and red became the norm when the clouds were not so dense as to preclude any sunset views at all. In London, people wrote of storm clouds glowing red half an hour after sunset (the acid veil reflected red light back towards the earth.) Artists were among the first to notice the change in colours, and curious Greek scientists have found that artists of the day used more red paint in 1816 and 1817 in their works than in other years. The most famous, William Turner, who was the 'Professor of Perspective' for Britain's Royal Academy of Art, and the country's highest paid artist, had secured a contract in Yorkshire to paint one hundred and twenty water colours across the county. He'd managed to do this in the brief fine–weather periods between the shocking weather, and he had recorded what he saw—brilliant colours.

Other creative people were at work also. Besides Mary Shelley, Jane Austin was working hard, and the weather, which she described in *Persuasion* fits the volcanic winter pattern well when, "… on a dark November day, a small thick rain almost blotting out the very few objects ever to be seen from the windows." Lord Byron wrote some iconic poetry named *Darkness* where, "… the bright sun was extinguish'd, and the stars Did wander sparkling in the eternal space..." Charles Dickens, who was a small child at the time, described continuous appalling weather in books like *A Christmas Carol* and *Great Temptations*. Some researchers suggest this showed Dickens remembered his childhood experiences of weather well, and others also suggest that his influence over the perception of what a winter should have looked like affects Britain even today. The early 1800 winters were particularly cold, and 'White Christmases' were the norm. Many modern people still expect to have them despite the fact that they have always been rare, except during cold periods.

The northern hemisphere winter of 1815—16 was unusually mild in North America. The veil was up of course, but at this stage, it was operating as a blanket, which allowed the seas and land to retain some of the heat gathered during the 1815 summer, absorbing some of the sun's energy, and radiating it as heat. In New England, there was very little snow, and residents of Maine allowed their heating fires to go out because it was so mild. The heating of the stratosphere was uneven—for example—the high northern latitudes were in complete winter darkness, whilst higher than normal air pressure over the Atlantic from the heating helped push back the cold arctic air, corralling it over the poles by walls of western wind. What scientists call the North Atlantic Oscillation was weakened, and there were few successful incursions of cold air into the middle latitudes during that winter.

Over in Europe, the weather became more unsettled, and some parts had as much as 80 per cent more rainfall than normal, including unusually high amounts of snow in the mountains. The same high–pressure area over the Atlantic that sheltered North America pushed the unsettled weather westwards. The autumn of 1815 was wet in central Europe and the higher rainfall and colder–than–usual temperatures during harvest time took their toll on the wheat harvests, and the price of wheat rose accordingly. This cheered the English as their harvest was good, despite the cold, but their joy didn't last long. The following winter, temperatures destroyed the crops of turnips they needed for cattle fodder. Snow, ice, and rain fell most days, and it never really got much better. As it was a time when communities were dependent on annual crops for survival, there was little stored in reserve. The delayed planting season of the 1816 summer, then regular storms that brought heavy rains, snow, or frosts during the growing season, meant disaster for farming communities. In Ireland, potatoes rotted in the flooded fields, wheat crops failed across Europe and the Americas, as did rice in China and India. Crop prices rose dramatically where scarcities arose, and livestock prices dropped just as dramatically because farmers had to sell their animals; they couldn't afford to feed them. John Post, the historian, says that Switzerland was hit the worst of all Europe, and that a pound of bread in 1817 cost more than the weekly wages of a hand spinner. Peasants starved and angry mobs stormed the bakeries and destroyed the shops. Desperate people fought with animals for scraps of food, ate the stinking corpses of starved livestock, and the leaves of nettles. Tens of thousands of people died in this, the "last great subsistence crisis" to face Europe. Some Swiss mothers were arrested and decapitated after they had killed their children, supposedly out of mercy, rather than see them starve. Others were saved by soup kitchens and the arrival of Russian grain from areas that had escaped the worst of the climate anomaly, and still others had managed to escape Europe for good, heading east to Russia or west to the United States.

The Battle of Waterloo had taken place in June 1815. More than fifty thousand young men were dead, and the English, under Wellington, as victors, were now required to maintain an occupation force in France and feed their soldiers until things settled down. By 1816, it became more and more difficult to find enough food, as the French crops had also failed. The grain that was available was expensive and poor quality. Wheat ground into flour was hardly worth buying. "You could not eat the bread. It stuck to the knife," said a Frenchman in 1817. Repatriated after the Napoleonic Wars, tens of thousands of men had returned home unemployed to France or England just as the food started to run out, and the price of bread skyrocketed.

Unemployment in post–war Britain reached 50 per cent. Disorder mounted, and soon there were riots in Dorset, Suffolk, Norfolk, and Wales, and though Tambora might not have been solely responsible, it was a sign of the times. In May 1816 in Cambridgeshire, civil unrest got so bad a demonstrator was shot dead, eighty people were arrested, twenty–four were convicted, and five were hanged! No one knew that the worst was yet to come.

In the United States, the North Atlantic Oscillation then brought cold fronts, which swept across the country in June, dropping temperatures as much as 20 degrees Celsius in minutes and delivering frosts and snowstorms in places that had had heat waves during the winter. In Canada, Quebec was as snow–bound as if it was still December and in Montreal ice, "as thick as a dollar" had frozen the newly planted crops. Newspapers heralded the coming famine.

And then came disease. Typhus arrived in County Mayo in Ireland in September just as hundreds of people began to wander the land as itinerant beggars carrying their lice with them. *Pediculus humanis* is a tiny louse whose parasitic relationships with humans probably started in the earliest days of our evolution. Typhus (*Rickettsia prowazekii*) however, is a nasty little bacterium that infects lice, and they in turn pass it on to humans by defecating in the wounds they make in our skin. When poverty rules, as it did in post–Tamboran Ireland, and people share clothing and blankets, the disease spreads quickly. Doctors estimated more than a million Irish men and women had contracted the disease and there may have been as many as one hundred and fifty thousand deaths by the time the outbreak finished in 1819.

To add to this loss, untold thousands left the country as pauper immigrants to seek better lives elsewhere.

In Asia, the summer of 1816 brought severe drought to the Indian subcontinent and southern China, particularly the populous Yunnan Province, rather than the usual monsoon. As crops failed, people starved or became weakened, and stagnant water sat in the sewers, ripe for diseases of all sorts. Then, in September, when the rains finally arrived, they came with a vengeance. There was severe flooding of the Ganges in India, as well as the Yangtze and Yellow Rivers in China, and thousands of people were drowned, building upon the tragedies brought by drought and famine. As thousands more starved, some parents sold their children or killed them to avoid watching them suffer. Farmers were destitute and looked around for a new lucrative cash crop. They found it in opium poppies, and its production spread from here to Thailand and Burma. This marked the beginning of the 'Golden Triangle' that still exists as the source of much of the world's opium today.

In 1816, cholera had been an endemic disease confined to the lower Ganges valley in India. It is a common

bacterium found worldwide in zooplankton and proto-
zoa, but now, with the human population so weakened
by drought, flood, and famine a strain emerged by chance,
which entered an increasingly mobile human population.
Cholera is a horrific disease, which takes life rapidly, and
stories of people dropping down dead in mid–sentence
are common. At one costume ball, partygoers collapsed by
the dozen on the dance–floor and were buried, I guess by
the host, in shallow graves in his back garden, still in their
masquerade clothing.

Cholera rapidly became epidemic and then pandemic,
spreading to Afghanistan and Nepal with the British army
and to Mecca and Medina with Moslem pilgrims. In
1819—20 it arrived in Bangkok, and soon bodies clogged
the canals and the river. In an ironic double whammy, it
also arrived in Java and the East Indies, killing over one
hundred and twenty thousand people in 1820, more than
Tambora had originally taken immediately after its eruption.
It then slowly moved eastwards and northwards, following
trade routes through the Philippines, Japan, and China,
and then Persia by 1822 and Moscow by 1823. Cairo lost
12 per cent of its population to cholera in 1824. It reached
England via France in 1831, where hundreds of thousands
of Frenchmen died, including the prime minister in 1832.
It also took hold in North America, entering via Montreal
and New York in 1832. The climate change brought about
by Tambora created conditions that helped cholera to spread
from the Bay of Bengal to the world, and it has taken tens
of millions of lives since then.

Tambora's effects on the weather lasted for three years.
Across the northern hemisphere, average surface temperature
in the 1816 and 1817 summers were well below normal,

and local climates were no longer predictable. Winter snow refused to melt and summer snow, which was brown in Hungary and red in Italy, terrified and astounded the locals as massive storm heads licked the ash from the stratosphere and brought it to earth.

Many people had no choice other than to move. In 1817 there were 22,240 climate refugees leaving their homes in Europe to head to America, Canada, or Australia. As an Australian, it is food for thought to think that some of the early settler families who came to Australia at this time may have come as a result of privations caused by Tambora. Certainly many of those convicted of minor crimes and transported to the early penal colony for their seven or fourteen year sentences would only have been 'criminal' out of desperation. What a different country it would be without these settlers in the early years. Australian descendants of convicts are proud of their heritage, but few may have realised their possible connections with a volcano on a small island to the north.

Some translocations weren't always successful—in Newfoundland, the authorities turned back eight hundred emigrants from Europe because of the lack of food. New England was pretty much all under cultivation by this time and farmed by established families who commonly had nine or ten children. The growing population was already putting pressure on the farms, and the failed crops of 1816 and 1817 were the final straw for many. Tens of thousands of people climbed into covered wagons and shifted to Indiana and Ohio and further west in scenes that have been replicated often by Hollywood movies. This 'land rush' created a 'real estate bubble' with intense land speculation. Easy loans left farmers vulnerable to any variation in prices of their products. Four new states were declared in the post–Tambora era—Alabama, Kentucky, Indiana, and Illinois. Farmers south of the snow line managed bumper crops in 1816—18 earning high prices on the European market because of the lack of produce there. But by 1818, as the climate stabilised and returned to normal in Europe, the European farmers were again able to produce food and prices the Americans were getting more than halved. With its rapid population increase, high debt and no way to pay it, the USA fell into its first major economic depression. Three hundred banks failed overnight in 1819. The destructive effect of Tambora's eruption lingered throughout 1819 till 1822 as warehouses full of grain rotted through lack of export demand.

The Smith family in Norwich, Vermont, suffered three failed crops in a row, and in a last ditch attempt to survive, Joseph, his wife, and nine children moved to an area in New York State well known for pious and devout communities. There, several years later his son Joseph Smith Junior said he had been visited by the angel Moroni on a number of occasions. Moroni, he claimed, showed him the location of some 2000 year old historical records. They were buried near his farm, and the young Joseph was happy to dig them up, translate them (because Moroni taught him how), and then publish them as *The Book of Mormon*. In 1830, thus started the Church of Jesus Christ of Latter–day Saints, also called the Mormon Church.

In January 1816, sunspots which were so large they could be seen with the naked eye had suddenly appeared after many years without there being any seen. That they could be seen for most of the day without eye protection was most unusual, but Tambora's dust cloud had dimmed the sun enough for people to be able to look directly at it. The connections seemed obvious to some, and easily attributed to the sunspot activity, and many debated the pros and cons of the argument endlessly. To the religious it seemed the day of judgement was soon to be upon them, and it seemed that God was dimming the sun and in time, He would blacken it entirely. Many people in Europe and America thought that it was God's will and, if He so wished it, good weather would return. In France, Britain, Sweden, and Italy priests were extolling their flocks to pray for dry weather and the cathedrals were full every day with the pious.

Some early 'environmentalists', such as Thomas Jefferson, warned that the climate was changing because of deforestation, an ominous concern that seemed before his time. Nowadays, there are many who are worried that our planet is becoming uninhabitable for similar reasons.

Italy was a fertile ground for prophets of doom. One astronomer in Bologna claimed the sunspots meant the sun would be extinguished by July 18th. This prophecy received a great deal of press coverage in America and Europe. The doomsayer became known as the 'mad Italian prophet' and his theory as the 'Bologna Prophecy'. Another man, a priest from Naples, made the papers claiming that Naples would soon be destroyed by a rain of fire that lasted four hours (perhaps an easy prediction to make considering Naples lies at the foot of Mt. Vesuvius, and scientists still say that it *is* likely happen sometime). Both these men were locked up for causing panic but too late as the hysteria had already spread. In England, *The Times* reported that, "The prediction of the mad Italian prophet, relative to the end of the world, had produced great dread in the minds of some, so that they neglected all business, and gave themselves up entirely to despondency." One woman committed suicide, and during a hailstorm, some residents of Lancashire were so sure of their impending annihilation they dropped to their knees in prayer.

In Austria, the fear drove the population of several villages to huddle together for protection, and the authorities, mistaking it for insurrection, dispatched troops to sort them out. In Ghent on July the eleventh, some frightened women were crowding into the church during a storm, and when the local cavalry sounded retreat at nine pm by blasting their trumpet as usual, some are said to have thought the sounds were from the Seventh Trumpet mentioned in the *Book of Revelation*, prophesising the end of the world: "... suddenly cries, groans, tears, lamentations, were heard on every side... three fourths of the inhabitants rushed forth from their homes, and threw themselves on their knees in the streets and public places."

In Germany, the crop failures and resulting famine also hit livestock hard; horses, for example, starved to death or otherwise became too emaciated to work. Necessity is the mother of invention, and the enterprising Baron Karl von Drais took the opportunity to invent what he called a *laufmaschine* or draisine, which became known as the *velocipede*. It was the first bicycle and made almost entirely out of wood. It had a simple design, and had no pedals. The riders had to sit on the seat and use their legs to run the bike, and at one time, a rider was recorded covering thirteen kilometres in an hour.

The results of the eruption were awesome: millions were affected; there was starvation, disease, and death; the destruction of the Tambora culture and people; massive European emigration; numerous floods and droughts; religious fervour and the creation of a new religion; the invention of the bicycle; the creation of magnificent art; the birth of science fiction and Frankenstein; widespread political instability; coloured snow and frosts in mid–summer—the list goes on.

I retold some of these stories to Sumbawans I met. Haqqul in Empang knew of few of them already; Saifal in Pancasila as the 'ranger', and whose business is Tambora, knew the basics but had several stories wrong (Napoleon did *not* lose because of Tambora); Ibu Maryam, the sultan's aunt, knew her local history and had had a teaching role through her museum to local school and university groups for many years, but her interests were more in the history of Bima and the succession of sultans over the years. Few others I met knew the importance of Tambora's eruption, and as of yet I had been unable to unearth any oral histories, or what I have always thought of as 'living memories' from Sumbawan families. There must still be some stories somewhere, I thought.

As a teacher, I also concluded teaching opportunities were being lost; children learning about their own history and the importance of it to the world would enrich the Sumbawan school education. But I think all of us can ponder on what it can tell us, or rather *warn* us, about the possible future effects of climate change, whether from natural causes or from the activities of our species. After all, if we could rerun history and exclude Tambora's eruption, the world might be a very different place.

Chapter 11

Back To Sumbawa

Whilst waiting to return to Sumbawa I found several resources that helped greatly in my understanding of what had happened nearly 200 years before. The first was a book by a father and son team: Nick Klingaman is a meteorologist, his father William a historian, and together they pulled off an unlikely triumph—a highly readable book containing history and high–level science and nearly 300 pages *about the weather!* Reading *The Year Without Summer: 1816 and the Volcano that Darkened the World and Changed History* gave me the answer to many of my questions and a greater understanding of the chemistry of the eruption.

In Indonesia *jam karet*, or 'rubber time' is often blamed for lateness or delays, and Iben and I were delayed several times before we could get back to Sumbawa. A small irony occurred on the day I had originally expected to be on the summit: I received in the mail a copy of Gillen D'Arcy Wood's new history of the Tamboran period called *Tambora: the Eruption That Changed the World*. Gillen Wood is an Australian university professor based at the University of Illinois in the US, and one area that greatly interests him is the interrelationship between people and the environment. Tambora is thus a fertile area for his research, and during the five–year journey of the writing of his book, he was able to uncover historical information from across the world and connect them, in a way no one had done before, to the calamitous events on Sumbawa in 1815. I had contacted him when I first heard about his new book, and he was enthusiastic and encouraging saying that he hoped large numbers of articles, books, and papers would soon be forthcoming as the world woke up to the importance of the eruption.

Professor Wood has become a champion of Tambora, and he enters the battle with her favour tied firmly to the lance of his research. He feels the eruptions of Vesuvius, Krakatau, and others are unfairly more famous. Tambora's eruption, he claims, was a "world– historical event" more akin to that of Thera on the Greek island of Santorini in 1628 BC, which is easily linked to the decline of the Minoan civilisation and to events retold in the Bible, such as the Israelites' exodus from Egypt. Also, if the mythical city of Atlantis really existed, Thera, with a VEI 6, could have been its destroyer. You get the impression that Tambora's relative exclusion to modern history is affronting to the professor and his book is an attempt to make things right. On this, he didn't need to convince me—I had already come to the same conclusion.

Wood had met Sumbawans who told folk stories of Tambora and the *zaman hujan au* (time of the ash rain). One story he retells is of a Tamboran king ruling the island from a palace of gold. They say his buried treasure is still in the forest, but the ghost of the king haunts it, embittered, twisted, and seeking revenge. He and the spirit of his beautiful daughter entice careless young men into the forest with the promise of riches and bliss and, they say, many have never been seen again. The real Tamboran king was called Raja Abdul Gafur. He lived in a wooden *kraton* in a reasonably wealthy small community, but it was never made of gold.

Gillen Wood's research had taken him further than any other I had read into the story of Tambora, and I learned much about the effects of the three–year volcanic winter in China, India, and elsewhere, and I suspect that his book will remain the definitive history of Tambora for a long time. He uncovered, translated, andpublished for the first time in English, for example, some wonderful Chinese poetry from a contemporary poet named Li Yuyang that brought tears to my eyes. In one, Li Yuyang describes in stark and haunting language some of the horrors faced by the people, and what they had to do for survival:

> *300 coins for a bag of grain*
>
> *300 copper coins for three days of life*
>
> *Where can the poor people find such money?*
>
> *They barter their sons and daughters on the streets.*
>
> *Still they know the price of a son*
>
> *Is not enough to pay for their hunger.*
>
> *And yet to watch him die is worse.*
>
> *Think of our son's body as food, as grain for one meal.*

The little ones don't understand, how could they?

But the older boys keep close, weeping.

Stop crying and go with him. Selling is a

blessing, because to buy you he must feed you.

The cold wind blows in their faces,

The parents wipe their tears away.

But back home they cannot sleep

While the birds moan like old men in the night

Li Yuyang

By the time I was finally preparing to return to Tambora I felt more empowered by knowledge. I had read all the accounts I could find of the eruption and anything about the history, geology, and biology of the region. I was excited to look at the mountain with fresh eyes and at last, at the end of May, I was on my motorbike heading east, back to Sumbawa. Iben had been delayed again, and as my window of opportunity for the trip was closing fast, I left a week before he was able to. He was going to start his *Tambora to the World* motorcycle trip to publicise the bicentenary, and he would be travelling from Pancasila through Indonesia, Malaysia, Thailand, Laos, and much of the rest of South East Asia. (The European part of his trip we had originally talked about had been shelved until more funding came through.) Iben was making a film, writing the story of his trip, and was nearly ready to go, but I just couldn't wait. He turned up at my place the afternoon before I left on a large brand new Kawasaki road trail motorbike he had bought through his sponsors. We discussed the timing, and as I had several stops I wanted to make in Sumbawa on the way, it was still possible that we'd be able to meet up and do the climb together. In the end, he was three days behind me, and we passed each other on the road as I was leaving.

My trip across Lombok to Sumbawa was easy and quick. A ferry was ready almost as I arrived, and the crossing was without incident. Before heading east in Sumbawa, I wanted to visit the mining town of Maluk, in the southwest corner of Sumbawa. Once, this small town had the distinction of having had one of the highest per capita incomes of any town in Indonesia at about almost USD 20,000 per annum. Newmont, the giant American mining company and a Japanese partner, Sumitomo, have the second largest gold and copper mine in the world called Batu Hijau, which means 'Green Stone', and it was located here. There used to be a large number of expatriates here, including enough families to support an International School also named Batu Hijau, and the local bar scene was famous, or perhaps infamous, with bars like the Kiwi Bar, the Trophy, and others plying their trade to thirsty miners. Along the main street, I saw an unusually high number of dusty, abandoned hair salons, which told a story of a more robust nightlife than there was here today, and I was sure it wasn't *the miners* getting their hair done.

To get there I followed the road south of the region's major town, Taliwang, famous for its spicy chicken (*Ayam Taliwang* can be found in *warungs* and restaurants all over Indonesia) and just kept going. Eventually the road climbs over a low range of hills, reaches the mine's gateway, and crosses its car park. Maluk is another two or three kilometres over the next hill. It is hot, dusty, and rapidly falling into disrepair. I found a hotel, which charged 300,000 rupiah for a room worth perhaps 100,000, and offered massages for 200,000 rupiah, three times the price of spas in Lombok.

Clearly being a wealthy mining town meant business owners could hike prices northwards as far as they liked.

But the town is a shadow of its former self. Nearly all the expatriates have gone now, and the few that are left are uncertain of their near future. By contract, the mine was supposed to be 51 per cent sold to Indonesian investors by the end of 2008. It wasn't, because the government didn't have the money it needed, and no other appropriate buyer could be found. The government took the company to an arbitration court hoping to sue for breach of contract but failed. A couple of years later, they demanded that Newmont build a smelter in Indonesia rather than ship their ore to China and also slapped a crippling export tax on the mine's copper products. Newmont claimed it was economically unfeasible, didn't make sense, and goes against the already agreed contract and refused to sign. The negotiations stalemated and production was almost at a standstill, their nine thousand employees have an uncertain future, and the town of Maluk was in danger of dying as all the service and supply industries that relied on the mine lost their income. Ironically, the West Sumbawa Regency, the local government, was also suffering—up to 80 per cent of its income came from the mine royalty program. They will have to resolve their problems to be mutually beneficial because the mine has a life of more than thirty more years if it is allowed to go ahead.

Maluk does have one lifeline, however, unrelated to mining. Located further south are a number of very popular surf beaches to which continuous streams of international surfers and backpackers head. Beaches with names like 'Supersuck', 'Sekongang,' and "Yoyo's" are famous among surfers, and they vie with Lakey Beach over in Dompu Regency for their attention. I rode out and had a quick look at some of the closest beaches and took a late afternoon swim, finding a number of lodges (that I wish I'd booked into rather than the one I had already paid for), and some handy beach–side food warungs. There is a stunning coastline here and the surf looked spectacular, so I have no doubt this will be a boom area of the future as more and more people realise that Bali has sunk under the weight of its own success and shun it for prettier places. I was just a passer–by, however, and after a quiet night in my expensive hovel, I jumped back on my bike and rode straight into the bright early morning sun towards Sumbawa Besar.

Sumbawa Besar is a small city of about sixty thousand inhabitants. Lying just across Saleh Bay from Tambora, the ash fall from the eruption completely destroyed the city in 1815, but the sultan rebuilt it, using slave labour, around 1820. It has a few interesting sites to visit but my first task on arrival was to buy petrol for the motorbike. I had ignored a petrol station on the way into the city, but after a fruitless search in town, I had to return to it—the only petrol stations the city has are on the highway that bypasses it.

It had taken me about four hours to get here from Maluk, and as it was just entering the heat of the day, I found a hotel on a hill overlooking the city. I checked in and tried to wait the heat out to emerge later in the afternoon, but impatient, I was back on the bike to explore the city in the heat, soon after one o'clock, and have lunch.

The Governor's house and the *kraton* are, as normal, located right in the centre of town, and they actually share the same city block. A high metal fence shielded them from the press of humanity, but the gate was open, and I rode in and parked under a tree beside a white two–story mansion, with locked louvered shutters on each of its windows. There wasn't a person to be seen anywhere. On the front wall, there is a brass plaque, which states in Dutch that this was the house of the Sultan of Sumbawa Besar. Two old Dutch cannons, strangely painted gold, glinted in the sun beneath two flagpoles. The Governor's residence, when he is in Sumbawa Besar, sits beside the kraton, and was easy to spot by its two official looking cars with flags on the bonnets parked in his open garage. There was no one here either.

I wandered over to the deer park. Every Governor's house or *kraton* that I have seen in Indonesia, from Medan to Bima, has a herd of deer in the garden and this one is no different. In Sumbawa Besar, the choice is *barking* deer, and they are certainly noisy. They live in an enclosure behind a metal mesh fence, and fifty–four of them came over to greet me. I sat in the shade eating apples for a while and feeding the cores to the boldest, who plaintively requested them, and I hung around the gardens for about an hour, but still saw no one—clearly both the sultan and the governor were not in residence, and their staff were taking full advantage of it.

The other major site of interest in Sumbawa Besar is the old palace. Called the *Istana Dalam Loka,* it is the largest wooden palace in the world. It shares a city block with the biggest mosque in town, a modern multi–level building with an old–fashioned tiled roof, unique hollow minarets, and glass doors.

I saw the *Istana* from the street and ended up parking and entering via a back gate. The palace was extraordinary. It was perched on teak tree trunks about three meters off the ground, with only one entrance—a rather unusual covered ramp at the southern end, designed to catch the breeze from the south. The whole construction reminded me of a giant sheep-shearing shed from New Zealand. I looked first around the gardens and found that they were well kept, but the whole effect was rather spoilt by meter–high white letters spelling out ISTANA DALAM LOCA running the length of the building like some cheap hyperbolic bling. The view was rather better from the front where the ramp descended, and I noticed a guard sitting at its top. I went up to talk with him and asked if the palace was open. The wooden doors behind him looked securely locked with large brass padlocks.

"If sir wishes to see inside," the guard replied in affected over–politeness, "then I shall open the door for him."

He then just pushed the door open—it hadn't been locked at all—and I went inside. Everything about the building is big. One enters a very large room called the Lunyuk Court, which was the major meeting room but now displays a number of photographs of royalty from early last century posing glass eyed for the camera, looking rather as they'd been stuffed. One photograph shows a large group of members of the *Sumbawa Jolly Jazz Club* from the 1930s. This group included a number of Europeans, whom I assumed to be Dutch and a big bass drum with their group's name inscribed on its skin. The next room is more of an empty hall fifty meters long with chambers off to both sides. The western side belonged to the king and his wives and includes a prayer room walled with netting and a chamber for the Ladies in Waiting. The eastern rooms were used by the married sons and their families. At the far end were the kitchens but these days nothing remains of them.

A ladder–like set of stairs rises up through a hole in the ceiling and I climbed up to have a look. The upstairs room runs the length of the building within the roof structure. A platform, which is raised more than a meter from the floor, follows the roof, and although there was no information, I suspected this might have been a sleeping platform back in the day, perhaps for servants or guards. Back downstairs, I wandered around a little more, noticing a few windows between the rooms with intricately carved wooden grills, but there was no furniture or anything else to give an impression of what life in the Istana had actually been like.

The Istana Dalam Loka is a strange building. Built in 1885, seventy years after the Tambora eruption, by the 16th Sultan of Sumbawa Besar, Sultan Mohammad Jalaluddin III, and it had fallen rather badly into disrepair by the time the new palace was built in 1932. In the 1980s, a Japanese team renovated it for posterity. I wondered if they had rebuilt it straight because these days the whole structure leans to the east, but it is designed to be flexible and earthquake proof, and the whole construction is without nails.

I went outside to talk to the obsequious guard at the front door and asked him what the government's plans are with the building. "One day, sir," he said, "maybe they will restore it to its former glory, but now there are many arguments. The sultan's family are in disagreement. Some will bring in furniture and the king's throne, and it will be a good tourist attraction then, sorry. People will be able to trace the past. Last year, they had some money, but it went to build a fence and an Islamic Centre next to the mosque. It will take more time. My apologies it is not ready for your good sir" Another visitor arrived and introduced himself. Iqbal was a native of Sumbawa Besar, but he said this was his first visit to the palace. He must have been past it a million times.

"Most people don't care about this palace," he said. "But they should, this is our history, yes?"

I asked the guard why the palace was elevated on stilts.

"Sir, the stilts are teak pillars, you must know. They came from all around this area. There are ninety–nine of them as this celebrates the ninety–nine attributes of God. The pillars put the king in a high position."

I guessed he meant by this that the king would be closer to God. Iqbal was impressed.

"Yes," he said. "We are all closer to God when we come here."

I left the two of them discussing religion and went back into town. I found a small supermarket and bought some supplies for the next day's travel and there, surprisingly, in a fridge were ice–cold cans of Bintang Beer—not what I had expected in this devoutly Islamic city. Happily resourced I retired to my hotel on the hill and watched the afternoon draw to a close, and the sun set somewhere over my family in Lombok.

The next morning, I left at dawn and took the road to Empang, Dompu, and Pancasila. The seasons had rolled on since my last visit, the corn had all been harvested, and the countryside was drying out. Now, much of the corn had been separated from their cobs and was spread out to dry on large concrete platforms. Huge orange piles of it were ready for package and export.

I stopped at the same seaside restaurant for a meal that Iben had brought me to in February and was warmly welcomed by the owner like an old friend. She again plied me with excellent coffee and I bought a packed lunch from her, with plans to eat it where I could sit and look at Tambora, then rode around the eastern parts of Saleh Bay, and turned west for the Sanggar Peninsula and the mountain I had come to see.

Riding along the coast of the Sanggar Peninsula I saw that the buffalo wallows I had stopped to photograph last time were still full with the giant beasts lounging amid their personal clouds of flies. I entered the grasslands and was glad to see the air was much clearer than in February, and I had great views of Tambora on my right as I rode along. The sea was on my left, and I was surprised to see Moyo Island just a few kilometres across the water. The February haze must have hidden it, as I didn't notice it the last time I had come through here.

Moyo Island guards the giant mouth of Saleh Bay. It's a small island compared to Sumbawa, but it still covers three hundred and forty–nine square kilometres and rises to more than six hundred and forty meters in height. The Indonesian government recognised its biological importance in 1986, and the result was the island became a nature reserve, and the waters off the entire south coast and most of the east and west coasts are a marine park now. In the true Indonesian way, being a National Park does not necessarily mean what it does in the west, because two thirds of the island was also a hunting park where people could shoot Timor deer and wild pigs and catch birds for the cage–bird industry. Well known for its birdlife, of the one–hundred and twenty–four species of birds found in Sumbawa, eighty–six of them are found on Moyo. Twitchers, as some varieties of bird watchers are called, come for thousands of miles to see rare species such as the yellow–headed parrot, the coral bird, and a type of megapod 'scrub turkey' called the tanimbar megapode which lives here too.

Megapodes build giant sand and mulch nests in which they bury a single large egg and then leave it to hatch alone, warmed by the rotting compost around it, and when it is ready, the chick digs itself out and fends for itself. We saw a nest off to one side of the road as we went past on the bikes but there had been no recent activity in it when I checked. Other birds were shy, it was after all the middle of a dry and hot November day, and we saw no mammals at all, but long–tailed macaques, wild cattle, pigs, barking deer, and twenty–one species of bat were all hiding in the forest somewhere The *Perama* tourist boats visit here on their Lombok–Komodo– Lombok route, and this is how many visitors arrive, but on our private sailing trip into Saleh Bay, we also stopped here overnight. Visiting boats moor off the Moyo coast out from the small village named Labuan Haji, which dominates a narrow beach on the western shore. The village boasts a school and a mosque, and has several little shops selling plastic rolls of single–dose shampoos, coffee mixes, and recycled plastic bottles of local, very sweet, honey. There are six small villages like this one on the island, containing perhaps a thousand residents who live by farming and fishing.

Having arrived in the evening, we were in earshot of the community sounds: the mosque, goats bleating, children playing, and someone's radio during the night. We could smell faint odours of fish being cooked and sambal, the ubiquitous chilli paste that brings tears to your eyes whilst it's being fried.

After breakfast, we piled into the yacht's rubber zodiac boat and went ashore via a short wooden jetty. Naked brown children frolicked in the shallows, their teeth as white as the sand in the bright sun, and they called "hello mister" repeatedly as we arrived. A number of keen local lads met us, ready to take us to the two waterfalls, known as *Brang Rea* and *Mata Staircase*, which are found in the forest along inland streams.

We negotiated a hire–price for the bikes, climbed on the back and were driven along dusty tracks past the school, with its sign advertising that it had been built with Australian aid funding, through five or more kilometres of farmland and into a forest for about a fifteen–minute ride. For a nature reserve, it sure took a while to enter the nature.

The waterfalls are stunning. We had to walk the last few hundred meters and could hear them well before we could see them. At Brang Rea, crystal clear water cascades over smooth limestone cliffs six or seven meters into a deep plunge pool. It was hot in the dusty dry forest outside, and we spent a happy hour leaping into it. It is a delightful place to swim, swing from some strategically placed ropes or leap from the heights into cool fresh water, and it was a contrast to the warm sea-water in which we had been spending a lot of time.

It has always amazed me how much effort I am willing to make to visit waterfalls. They must touch something deep in my psyche and I suspect I am not alone. Celebrities like Princess Diana and Mick Jagger visited (though I suspect not at the same time) and made them a famous holiday destination. The locals complained of the times when VIPs visit, saying that all the forest tracks and the waterfalls had to be closed to anyone outside of the VIP party for several days. Any visitors on *Perama* boats or plebeian yachts like ours that arrived during these times miss out on visiting the waterfalls and the locals miss out on much needed income.

Princess Dianna didn't come by boat, of course. She would have used a seaplane or a helicopter, and she stayed at the other famous secret of Moyo Island: there is a resort in a bay on its south western coast. Amanwana Resort is a five star tent hotel on a private beach. We motored past in the Zodiac to take a look, but certainly weren't welcome to go ashore and sticky beak. Well–heeled tourists come here for quiet and solitude and spend their days snorkelling or SCUBA diving on magnificent coral reefs or lounging around reading, and perhaps wander up through the jungle to the waterfalls for an hour or so. Some go deer shooting.

The reviews of the resort read well online. One recent visitor on *Trip–Advisor* said:

> "I love staying in luxury tents. This remote luxury tented camp on Moyo Island, Indonesia is one of my favorite places in the world. You take a short 45 min— hr sea plane flight from Bali over the island of Lombok and the volcano and land on the sea pulling up to the dock at Amanwana. What a way..."

This sounds great until you read the negative reviews. For example, you are not allowed on the beach unless you have booked a front row tent, and this really wound some guests up. It was also misleading because there were speedboat operators in the village of Labuan Ai Bari on Sumbawa who could get you there in thirty minutes. This was the route to the island of package tours and several companies picked people up in their hotels in Sumbawa Besar in the morning and arranged day trips for snorkelling, waterfall hikes or even to visit the bat caves found somewhere in the jungle. Moyo is off the beaten track but perhaps worth more than just a quick look: after all, as one mangled–English tourist brochure puts it:

> "White sand that makes the beach in Pulau Moyo looks very beautiful, the waves are rushing after the beach, and accompanied by a twilight which made the atmosphere becomes more romantic; powerful eliminate all the fatigue after the adventure."

My view of Moyo Island from the peninsula petered out as I approached Calabai, the largest town of this part of Sumbawa.

Calabai is a timber town and some 20,000 hectares of the Tambora forest is open to the loggers. I noticed several large high schools, a number of mosques, and areas of markets and shops, which suggest the population of this otherwise sleepy town must be reasonably high. Calabai is on the coast and was a close neighbour of my destination Pancasila, so I just followed the road through it and rode up the hill.

Chapter 12

Pancasila

I had almost arrived in Pancasila about mid-afternoon, but heavy rain started, so I pulled off the road and sheltered in a derelict house for more than an hour. The coffee plantations were everywhere along this part of the hill, and coffee bushes surrounded the house. It was only a kilometre or so short of the village, but it had a serviceable veranda to sit on, and a dry place to park my motorbike. As the rain intensified, I was joined by a couple of other motorcyclists with whom I shared my lunch, and together we tut–tutted over the misfortune of getting caught in the rain. Later I discovered the real value of this stop, besides staying dry, was in learning that there was good phone reception there because there was none in Pancasila only a short distance up the road. I could easily return here to phone my family.

In Pancasila itself, Pak Saiful had finished the guesthouse rooms I had seen being built in February and his wife Ibu

Bahri, opened one for me when I pulled in. Saiful was out, but he recognised me as soon as he came home and asked about Hughen and Iben. We talked about climbing Tambora and employing a guide. "Guides cost 200,000 rupiah a day if they are experienced. New local people will work for 150,000 rupiah. If you are alone, you should take two, one can be a porter also."

He called out to a young bloke to go and fetch the guide whose turn it was.

"We have about fifty guides and porters here," he said, "so they all take it in turns."

Very soon, two young men arrived. They were small and wiry and at least half my weight. Arman would be the guide leader, and Herman the porter. I asked Arman how many times he had been to the summit. "Happy," he said, misunderstanding me. I tried again, with what I hoped was clearer Indonesian.

"No, how many times? Not 'how do you feel?'"

"Ah," he said. "Many!"

This was the start of our relationship. I would always have to repeat my sentences and usually have to ask him to repeat his. Neither the twenty year old Arman, nor Herman who was older than his friend at twenty–one spoke any English. Our accents were so different it was difficult for us to communicate without concentrating really hard. However, they seemed like nice guys, and we agreed we'd leave at seven am the next day if they'd come to the guest house about half an hour before to pack and get ready.

After they had gone, I went to watch the village soccer game in the paddock in front of the guesthouse. It was Pancasila verses Garuda, and it was a keen competition, with the teams putting in tremendous athletic efforts on a rain–soaked rough village green. The goals were half–size, and I watched from the end where the goalie was ankle deep in water. The village children found me a novelty, and a crowd of giggling kids gathered around. Many wanted their photos taken, and even some of the parents asked me to photograph them with their babies, thanking me profusely afterwards. Pancasila won the game two–one, and as it was getting dark, people quickly dispersed to their homes, and I retired to the guesthouse veranda.

Pak Saiful arranged a dinner for me of salty fried chicken, rice, and some boiled vegetables and sat and talked as I ate. One of the results of the wet season is that the trail to Post 1 was overgrown and crossed by fallen trees. It is cleared during the dry season and it is possible to ride to the *Pos 1* by trail bike. This cuts off eight kilometres of the hike each way, saving six hours of walking. Some of this trail is hard greasy clay when it is wet and so slippery it is hard to walk on, let alone stay upright on a bike.

So, the bad news for me was that my hike would be sixteen kilometres longer than I had expected. Saiful asked me if I was sure I really wanted to climb Tambora.

"It has been raining everyday for a week. It will be very slippery, and the leeches will be bad. And you are already old," he said. "It is a very hard climb."

"You cheeky bugger," I replied. "How old are you?"

Nearly all the climbers of Tambora these days are university students. I guess older people are a greater risk—rescues would be a very tricky thing to organise. The mountain was not exactly a walk in the park, and Saiful was the man who organises them. Saiful, no doubt, was looking at me wondering how they could carry me out with a broken leg, weighing more than double the local blokes. But my only concern was the quality of my boots. I had bought them cheap in Lombok for 250,000 rupiah. They are undoubtedly a pirated brand copy, and even on the flat, they didn't feel particularly comfortable. I told Saiful that if they gave me blisters, I would return quickly. Already old indeed!

I then asked to see the registration book again, or "guest book" as he called it, and I looked at it in more depth than I did in my first visit to Pancasila. I counted the climbers. Already one hundred and twenty–two people had climbed in 2014, including just ten foreigners—two each from Canada and Brazil, four from Belgium, and two Malaysians, who were up there that very night.

In 2013, there were six hundred and eight climbers of which twenty–four were foreigners from Malaysia, Holland, Canada, Bulgaria, Australia, Poland, Singapore, Russia, Germany, England, Brazil, and Switzerland. All the rest were groups of university students from Indonesia. The largest group included seventy–one climbers, though groups of between ten and twenty were more usual.

Tambora was clearly barely on the radar for foreign tourists but well in the sights for Indonesians. There was only me going up the next day, albeit with two guides, so we were going to have the summit to ourselves—a rare luxury on our crowded planet.

I asked Saiful if he knew anything about the archaeo-logical diggings of the old village of Tambora and if it was worth going to the site to have a look around.

"You can go there, it's about five kilometres. There's not much to see," he replied, "just jungle."

"Let's have a look anyway when I come back down," I suggested. "You have to walk. With all this rain the road is too slippery to ride motorbikes."

Saiful was clearly not keen to go, and a ten kilometres return walk just after a 41 kilometre mountain climb didn't seem like something I was really going to want to do, so I let the idea slide. Anyway, I thought, perhaps it was best not to make a tourist attraction of an archaeological dig until it was officially opened and protected. It may be an extremely interesting place to see one day.

When the volcanologist Haraldur Sigurdsson, researchers from the University of North Carolina, and the Indonesian Directorate of Vulcanology excavated one of the Tambora houses in 2006, they made headlines. Ibu Maryam in Bima had mentioned Sigurdsson to me, but he was already famous worldwide. As a professor from the University of Rhode Island, he was a lead author of the *Encyclopaedia of Volcanoes* and the star of a TV program called *The Riddle of Pompeii.* Sigurdsson has had an exciting career in exotic places across the world from Hawaii to his native Iceland, including more than twenty years returning to Tambora on fieldwork. I was unable to reach the 75 year old to ask him about their find, but the media had already done it for me: quotable quotes come from important people and numerous websites list some of Sigurdsson's. He spoke in headlines when he said, "There is potential that Tambora could be the *Pompeii of the East,*" and this naturally fired the imaginations of journalists everywhere, so for a year or two Tambora Village had a moment in the sun.

Sigurdsson was clearly excited and the 'great cultural' interest of a two hundred year old unknown kingdom, undisturbed and sealed beneath a layer of ash and pumice, created ripples worldwide. In his 2006 excavation of a single house, he found two bodies. They were adults who were carbonised instantly by temperatures that were close to

900 degrees Celsius in a pyroclastic flow, and they had been buried under three metres of dust and pumice and rock. One clutched a large knife, perhaps in a puny attempt at protection, although as she was lying next to the cooking pots and the hearth of her fire, perhaps she was just cooking, oblivious to her impending doom. The archaeologists found bronze bowls, clay pots, fine china, metal spice grinders, and numerous other artefacts that linked the Tamboran culture to the Khmer cultures of Cambodia and Vietnam, and they concluded from the quality of the goods that the Tamborans were a wealthy people. They were known to have spoken a different language to the Bimanese and the Sumbawans, and it was probably a Mon–Khmer language related to others still found in South East Asia today but, as Sigurdsson said, "The explosion wiped out the language. That's how big it was," and "we're trying to get these people to speak again, by digging."

Local villagers had been finding old pottery shards and fragments of bone in a jungle erosion gully, about five kilometres from the coast, that had cut through the volcanic rock and they showed them to Sigurdsson when he was conducting research on the volcano in 2004. There was clearly something of interest buried under the volcanic debris, and Sigurdsson came back with ground–reading radar equipment and a team of archaeologists. It was then a relatively simple matter to locate the 6 x 10 metre house and carefully dig. Sigurdsson said, "All the people, their houses, and culture are still encapsulated there as they were in 1815. It's important that we keep the capsule intact and open it very carefully."

Rik Stoetman, an expatriate Dutchman who managed several expeditions of volunteers to the village site, helped with the digs. His photographs of the skeletons and the domestic equipment found in the houses are poignant–coiled ropes, pottery, *keris* knives, pots of carbonised rice and bamboo shades, and the skeletons, all unearthed after two centuries, revealed a story of what life in the village must have been like.

Perhaps a future dig will even find Raja Abdul Gafur himself and, if so, the world will no doubt hear about it: digging up kings always creates headlines. In the 2008 season, the archaeologists led by Dr Geria of the Bali Institute for Archaeology uncovered a second house within which a single male skeleton was found sitting upright. He may have been smoking when he died as he still had with him a copper tobacco box. A ceremonial spear lay by his side. He wore jewellery: rings, a bracelet, and a pendulum necklace. These suggested to the experts that he might have been part of the royal family, although not the king himself.

In 2009, another house was uncovered, and a man's skeleton was found lying outside the door. He had died protecting his head with his hands.

The Indonesian government took the lead to ensure that the digs were carefully done, and who knows, maybe it *will* be the "Pompeii of the East". However, according to Rik Stoetman, the government's feeling now is that if the findings cannot be preserved properly because of the isolation of the site, the cost of preservation, or the security of the whole process then perhaps it is better to leave everything in the ground until the country can afford to ensure the village's safety. Therefore, it might take many years for all the secrets of the village of Tambora to be revealed.

I certainly agreed that it was better to leave it alone if it couldn't be properly dug up, because elsewhere in the world I had seen what leaving known archaeological sites alone could bring about. Near Nazca in Peru, for instance, locals regularly go on treasure hunts in the desert looking for gravesites to open and empty of their treasures, leaving the mummified occupants exposed to the elements for the first time in a thousand years. Tourists like me are left wandering around and looking at the pillaged pits and regretting what the present takes at the expense of the past. For poor communities, this was an irresistible source of improving circumstances, and I feared that villagers around Tambora would develop a taste for the 200– year–old pottery and ancient *keris* knives, which could turn a nice profit on the black market or even just to the tourist trade. Village farmers, already handy with a pick and shovel, could easily mine the ancient village without anyone disturbing them—the official digs lasted only a few weeks of each dry season, and locally employed labour handled much of the heavy digging in those weeks anyway. In fact, I wondered whether I would be offered any artefacts by the locals as I wandered around Pancasila but happily I wasn't—yet. Instead, villagers eagerly posed on the steps of their stilted houses for photographs or waved cheerily from motorbikes and minivans as they passed.

The increasing numbers of climbers of the mountain and paid work in coffee plantations brings good revenue into the village. However, there are many other people living on the slopes of Tambora and many mouths to feed. The old story has a predictable ending but I really hope the site remains secure until it can be properly opened up.

Chapter 13

Tambora

We left as planned just after seven in the morning. Arman and Herman had turned up on time, and we loaded the packs with instant noodles, rice, coconut biscuits, and bottled water. Saiful suggested that I bought and drank my water from bottles, even though the first three posts have spring–water sources very close. He said foreigners often get a sick stomach from the local water, but it was what the guides would be drinking. Since I didn't have to carry the bottles, I agreed and bought some, though in the end I needed to drink the spring water as well and had no adverse side effects.

The first eight kilometre stage, from Pancasila to *Pos 1*, is reasonably simple. We set off through lush coffee planta-tions, shaded by huge trees along the roads I had ridden in February to visit the Hindu temple. It took us forty minutes to reach the path that disappears into the jungle

I had seen then, and we plunged into the forest. Its gloom closed around us, and I was thrilled to see what looks like undisturbed rainforest. But it is a remnant patch because soon we were on what was once a cleared roadway, used initially by loggers who selectively cut out the biggest trees and then by government workers who had run a water pipe through the jungle from a mountain spring to the village. The path roughly follows this water pipe all the way to the first designated rest area called *Pos 1*.

The walking here was not strenuous, but the thick undergrowth made it painful; the path now overgrown with bracken ferns, fishbone ferns, and raspberry bushes. Saiful had said that in the late dry season it was usually possible to be driven this stretch all the way to *Pos 1* on a trail bike, but climbing over fallen logs and slipping on hard clay that offered little grip to my boots, I could see why we couldn't ride it this early in the season.

We pushed through the ferns which were dripping with the morning dew and from yesterday's rain and that, combined with sweat, soon meant I was dripping wet myself. Being much bigger than my guides meant I walked face–first into the spiders' webs that were above their heads and had to push through the vegetation on both sides of the track which they could slip through easily, barely touching them. The raspberry bushes, which look like their relatives the climbing roses, hide their branches and thorns among soft fern fronds at just the right height to ensure I blundered into them and within minutes, my forearms were bleeding from their scratches.

The track gently sloped up, and we were climbing a little at every step. My boots were comfortable enough so far, and I didn't think I was going to be troubled by blisters, so I felt all was right with the world when we arrived at *Pos 1* and stopped for an early lunch.

This post is a clearing in the undergrowth of the forest, which has a *barugaq* (a tin–roofed wooden shelter) with a raised platform to sit on and a fireplace for cooking. We checked our feet for leeches. I hadn't yet seen any on the path, but Arman, who was wearing open rubber thongs[1] on his feet had a number of fattened leeches among his toes which were already swollen with his blood. Herman, who like me was wearing boots, escaped the bloodsuckers, but I found three or four trying to squeeze through my socks. A couple had managed a bite, and I pulled them off quickly—amazed that I hadn't felt a thing.

Leeches are interesting animals. They are oligochaetes, like earthworms, and hermaphroditic. They have a sucker on each end, so they can be difficult to pull off. When they bite, they introduce an anti–blood–clotting agent into the blood called hirudin, and the wounds they make can bleed for several hours. There are more than seven hundred species known, and Europeans used one of them for several thousand years up to the 19th century, for bloodletting as a medical procedure. Some species are very large: once, when I was traveling in Nigeria, I heard of a man who had fallen asleep drunk in a ditch one night to be fatally attacked by leeches and drained of his blood. The story told was that there were only nine leeches involved!

The Tambora species didn't seem so life–threatening, luckily, but they made up for it by their high numbers. I watched as Arman took out a little bottle of brown liquid and doused his leeches with it until they let go. The liquid

---

1   Thongs (Australia) are rubber sandals (USA), 'flip flops' (UK), 'jandals' (NZ)

was his invention: a pungent concoction of cigarette ash and tar. I was intrigued and later tried it on a leech on my own foot but was never convinced of its effectiveness—removal of leeches was a revolting thing to have to do and pulling them off quickly or scraping them off with a knife seemed to be the best way to make them let go. People have used burning cigarettes or matches, salt, disinfectant, and other substances, but these increase the danger of the leech vomiting up its stomach contents into the wound, which could then get infected. As it is, the bites can be itchy and take weeks to heal, and it takes even longer for the marks to disappear.

Arman and Herman busied themselves lighting a fire, using plastic rubbish left behind by previous groups as kindling, and soon they had rice and instant noodles on the boil. I watched Herman splitting branches to get smaller dry pieces to burn. At one point, he cut his finger, and to stop the bleeding, he immediately picked up some dirt from the ground and rubbed it into the cut—a mud poultice. It didn't seem particularly hygienic to me, but he wasn't bothered by the cut again on the trip.

The *Pos 1* spring was only a few meters away and was, in fact, a gap in the pipe that provided the town's water supply. Water entered a tank and then ran into another, clearly the pipe we had followed, back down the hill to Pancasila.

After lunch, we set off for *Pos 2* and the climbing started in earnest. The path was blocked by numerous fallen trees which we either had to climb over or crawl under and a number of very steep sections both up and down through small valleys. The path is narrow and overgrown with many roots and vines, and the most annoying vine–like clumping palm, which Arman calls *duli,* ready to trap the unwary. Duli has thousands of hooks and thorns, and it latches onto any clothing or skin that passes by. Because the fronds are long, you can walk a few meters before it makes you stop, and it takes a few minutes to unhook. Leeches were everywhere, and any pause like this made me feel more vulnerable.

It took us an hour and a half to reach *Pos 2*, which was another tin–roofed *barugaq*. The people who lugged the tin and timber up here were hardy people indeed; it was not something you will ever see me doing. The *Pos* was next to a fast flowing stream and there was a nice flat, cleared place to pitch a tent. We stopped for a rest and to pull off the leeches that had managed to grab hold as we had passed them. As soon as I sat in the *barugaq* I could see a few more inching their way towards us across the ground.

From here, the track rises to *Pos 3* with a number of long inclines that took us another hour and a half to climb. There were many more logs to climb over or under, some very slippery sections of the trail to navigate, and a million more leeches to avoid. Just before we arrived, the skies opened, and heavy rain thundered through the forest. It wasn't yet cold, and the exertions of the climb had made me so wet already the rain was actually very pleasant.

Pos 3 was our destination for the day and was the usual camping site for two–day treks. The clearing for tents here is large and open, and there is another tin-roofed *barugaq*. The water source is about 200 meters off to one side on a narrow path. You can see the crater rim from here lit up in the afternoon if the air is clear.

Most visitors doing the trek in two days rise at midnight and leave at one am to climb to the summit for sunrise, and this was our plan too. It was cool here but not cold. The forest surrounding the clearing is dense and ferns pressed in on each sid. Among the ferns were little red-flowering plants which released annoying sticky seeds on our clothing when we brushed past them. Huge trees shade the clearing. From the viewpoint of a large log, I watched as low clouds moved slowly through the valley beside us. We had walked just over fourteen kilometres in six hours, mainly up, so I was happy to stop, pull off the last of the leeches, and change into dry clothes.

It was mid–afternoon, and in the *barugaq* already, sheltering from the rain, the Malaysian couple I had seen listed in the registration book and their guides were cooking lunch and waiting for the rain to stop. They had spent the day on the summit and said it had been very hot up on the crater's edge because they hadn't arrived until the sun was already high, but the views were spectacular. The guides offered us coffee they prepared on a gas stove, and as the rain cleared, they packed up, threw all their rubbish onto the ground around the *barugaq*, including the empty gas containers, and then headed downhill. I heard later that they arrived exhausted well after midnight, but as we cleared up their mess and carried their rubbish that wouldn't burn downhill for them, I didn't have much sympathy.

I pitched my tent and lay in it for a while feeling decadent as Arman and Herman collected water, built the fire, and cooked the meal of instant noodles and rice. We sat close to the fire to eat, chatting amiably. I tried a bit of bush philosophy with Arman.

"When that log over there fell, if there was no one here to hear it, do you think it made any noise?"

"Of course," he replied, looking at me as if I was an idiot. I gave up—I had run out of Indonesian words to go further anyway.

Darkness fell quickly, and I was in bed by about 7.30, folding my single blanket in two to get as much warmth as

I could. Arman and Herman used thin fleece sleeping bags, and they slept in the *barugaq*; although as it got colder, I could hear them talking quietly, and I doubted they had much sleep at all.

At midnight, they were up preparing breakfast—instant noodles and rice again. Herman brought me some coffee, and I was up raring to go with an apparent burst of energy that was more bluster than real—I could easily have stayed in bed. At one o'clock we started the climb to *pos 4* and *pos 5* and then to the summit. It was pitch dark, on a moonless night, but our headlights were enough to follow the path.

From this level up, Tambora has another challenge—stinging nettles. These charming little plants of the genus *Urtica* give painful burning stings at the slightest touch. Nettles are infamous plants in history whose nastiness belies their usefulness. For instance, they are medicinal plants used for the treatment of arthritis and gout, rheumatism, haemorrhage, flu, and dandruff. They are the sole food species for numerous species of butterfly larvae; the young leaves are an excellent source of vitamins A and C, iron, potassium, manganese, and calcium when eaten or drunk as a tea, and the German army wore uniforms made from their fibres during the First World War cotton shortage.

The nettles press in on both sides of the path for much of the way up the long ridges to *Pos 4* and as far as *Pos 5*. They grow larger here than I have ever seen before—some are nearly three meters tall and in places, they are the dominant plant in the understory. Arman called them *pajatan,* and they are indeed painful, even with a slight brush against the skin (in fact they are more with slight brushes—if you 'grasp the nettle' strongly, the stinging hairs get less of a chance to sting). The stinging lasts about ten minutes or so before fading, but the skin can get red blotches for a while. Their tiny, odourless flowers cluster and hang down in thin stems, about head height, and soon my forehead was burning as I walked into them in the dark. Arman nimbly escaped any contact with them at all, and I don't think he believed me when I told him they were nothing compared to the Australian Stinging Tree—which can hospitalise a victim.

We were at *Pos 4* by about three o'clock. It was just a clearing between very tall and straight trees surrounded by the *pajatan* nettles. Here at night it was cold. There was no *barugaq* or water source, so few people camp here, and we just stopped for a short rest. Then, soon after leaving *Pos 4,* we came across a log, about twenty meters long, which was used as a bridge across a very thick area of nettles. I found my boots had no grip at all on its slippery surface and shuffled very gingerly along its length. At one point, my feet went out from under me and, of course, I fell into the nettles. I was even stung through the material of my trousers.

The track keeps rising steeply, and breathing became more difficult for me with the increasing altitude. It was tiring, and I started to stop to take short breaks more and more, wondering why I was labouring so much when Arman, who was doing the whole climb wearing his trusty red rubber thongs, didn't even appear to be sweating. His only condescension to the cold had been to don two pairs of green socks, which had individual toe sockets like gloves.

We stopped at *Pos 5* for an extended rest, and Arman lit a fire for warmth. It was extremely cold, but the exertion of the climb meant my shirt was wet enough from sweat that I was able to wring out a cupful of liquid. We huddled around the fire, and I tried to dry out, but I quickly started to get cold nevertheless and wondered at the delay. Arman's intention was to time our departure to the summit just right so that we would arrive there as the sun broke over the horizon, and we therefore left just before five am.

Casuarina trees became the dominant tree species at this altitude, and the forest opened up to include grasses: first the *alang–alang* grass people used to thatch the roofs of their houses and then stronger tussock grasses. At one point, we heard a large animal crashing off though the undergrowth, and the fresh digging in the earth around the path told me it was most likely a wild pig. In the predawn stillness, I could hear the first tentative chirpings of a number of bird species preparing to join the dawn chorus.

The path soon becomes very steep, and the trees begin to peter out, and then even the grass becomes rare. After nearly two hours, we arrived on a high plateau, a flat barren landscape of weathered rocks and volcanic dust cut by crevices and tortured rock outcrops. There is little vegetation, but the local edelweiss plant (*Anaphalis* sp) is common, but it was unfortunately not in flower during my visit. Also, there was a small white flowering plant that looked like a cushion that I have seen in New Zealand, where alpine plants like this grow impressively large. People there called it a "vegetative sheep".

The Tambora plateau lasts for several hundred meters, and the sun rose above the horizon as we crossed it. The summit was another half hour away on our right, but it was the crater that I wanted to see. I hurried over to the edge, in such excitement I received a warning shout from Arman, who was worried I was about to go tumbling off the edge.

The scene was awe–inspiring. The crater was so vast no photo could ever do it justice. Clouds mostly covered the bottom when I was there, but every now and then, it cleared enough to see areas where steam and gas are still seeping from the earth. I could see a green lake, but the sense of scale looking down from the top was so out of kilter that I had no idea if it was large or small.

From the top edge of the crater, it was seven or eight hundred meters to the floor. I realised that the one and a half kilometres of the mountain that was blown off the top in the eruption, was actually well over two kilometres if measured from the crater floor. Two hundred years ago, I would have had to keep climbing for several hours more to reach the summit.

Looking down at what once must have been a veritable pit of hell during the eruption, I reflected on the chaos it had created. Unknown outside the East Indies, it was the secret killer, a tectonic assassin intent on reaping lives from across the world. But now it seemed to be no threat at all—there are no churning, bubbling lava pools, or lakes of boiling mud like you see on other volcanoes. The rocky crater floor was still seeping gas—clouds of it rise and shift in the breeze, but it was silent, at least from where we were at top of its crater. The green lake looks innocuous, as if we'd be able to paddle in its shallows. Tambora was no Hades and there was no Cerberus keeping us from entering (or perhaps escaping), but it sat there in magnificence. The only guards to this crater were the leeches and the thick bands of *pajatan* nettles. Tambora was revealed to me as just a mountain, glorious indeed, but blameless for its excesses of two centuries ago.

The sunrise was magnificent, and the early morning light made the crater walls glow and change colour by the minute. Rock falls started as sun warmed the walls, and I could hear them almost continuously for the rest of the time we were up there.

We stood on the north western edge of the crater, and I looked across to the other side, seven kilometres away. The circular crater's circumference of twenty–one kilometres is impressive, and it is a clearly visible pockmark that can be seen from space.

Looking west, I could see Mount Rinjani on Lombok in the distance, blue in the haze and rearing above a layer of cloud. My family was there, readying for school and getting on with their lives. I was sorry there was no phone service from the summit: it would have been fun to phone.

Looking down there was Moyo Island, and closer still to Sumbawa, a small island named Satonda in the northwest. We had visited this beautiful little island on our sailing trip from Lombok to Komodo several years earlier; a small volcanic caldera, which has a very salty and nearly circular lake within it.

Satonda is so well known to travellers that even the rich and famous end up there too. In fact, a magnificent 75–metre super–yacht dropped anchor at the island the same time as we did, and we watched as its sides opened like garage doors and several rubber zodiacs zoomed out as if it was a rehearsed scene from a James Bond movie.

"Look, that ship's having babies" said my five year old son, Harry. It was the *Ocean Victory*, one of the world's top 50 super— yachts at the time (I know because I looked it up on our return). An "unnamed Russian oligarch" whom we actually met on the island owned it, but the man clearly wished to remain aloof from us. Some of his twenty–one crew, who were mostly New Zealanders and friendlier than their boss, had carried small canoes for his two children to paddle on the lake. The Russians were oblivious to the biology of the lake and just wanted to have fun, but the high salinity of the water creates a unique habitat that was dominated by stromatolytes. Stromatolytic reefs were common in the Pre-Cambrian and Early Palaeozoic oceans and were important sources of our petroleum these days, so scientists like to study Satonda's lake to learn about "foraminifera and mats of in-situ calcifying microbes of cyanobacteria" as one paper put it.

Satonda was uninhabited, but there were a few cabins for visitors to hire if they wished to stay a while, and when we were there they were being dressed up for a wedding party due to arrive in a day or two. Most visitors to Satonda came by small boats from the town of Calabai on the coast of Sumbawa—an easy thing to arrange and an obvious addition to the volcano climb experience.

Some locals talk about Satonda actually having no lake until Tambora's eruption, and the caldera was filled by a tsunami and, they say, it has stayed full until today. It was possible, and evaporation would explain its high salinity, but 200 years is a long time. I'd expect the water from a tsunami would have enough time to have completely evaporated by now—it was clearly being replenished from somewhere as the water level marked the beginning of the forest, thus showing it hadn't changed for a long time. I suspected the lake may well have existed before Tambora's eruption as cold craters often have lakes. Today the forest grows up the sides of the caldera and blankets the outside of the cone. Thousands of large fruit bats make their home in it, and the skies darken as they leave their roosts before sunset to fly across the narrow straits to the fruit–laden Sumbawa and the slopes of Tambora, which were clearly visible to the southeast.

We had scrambled up the western slopes to a viewpoint where I took photographs of our tiny yacht under the hulking Tambora, flat topped and exhausted in the distance. Now, feeling pretty exhausted myself and standing looking back the other way, I could see where we had climbed that day. How tiny it all looked.

It was amazing how quickly the day warmed up. The sun was above the horizon for less than thirty minutes before I had removed all my cold weather gear, and my shirt had started to dry. The Malaysians I had met at *Pos 3* had mentioned the heat, but they hadn't been here for dawn, just during the day, so I knew it would soon become uncomfortably hot as there was no shade or shelter of any kind on the crater rim. Tambora's summit was never a hospitable place; therefore it was quickly time for us to leave and to start the descent back to Pancasila.

Chapter 14

The Descent

I wasn't looking forward to going down. It meant a twenty-one kilometre, twelve-hour slog all the way back to Pancasila, and my feet were already sore, though luckily not blistered. My leg muscles ached with the exertions of the climb up, and I was hungry. Rice and instant noodles, it seemed, are not sufficient fuel for a big bloke such as me—I was quickly becoming a shadow of my former self.

But it was very different following the trail down towards *Pos 3* in daylight. I got my first splendid views of the hills and valleys on either side of the trail we had passed in the dark and some of the substantial drops on each side of the narrow trail. A slight breeze had come up, the *Casuarina* trees whispered and moaned in delight, and we passed between them. The trees were full of small birds that sang and cavorted about, and at one point, I saw some tracks in the sand next to the trail.

"Babi?" I asked Arman "Pigs?" "No," he replied. "Kijang." *Kijang* are deer. I didn't see them, but these were most likely rusa deer (*Cervus timorensis*), which are found across much of the Indonesian archipelago. The same species makes rather tasty prey for the komodo dragons on their island lair not far to the east, but up here, they are safe from predators, except perhaps for the odd human deer hunter. (Rusa deer, incidentally, were introduced by people to Komodo over the past thousand years, so neither they or even today's population of Asian water buffalos, which the dragons also enjoy, were the original prey of the komodo dragons during their evolution. That honour goes to two other species, which explain why the komodo dragons grew to be so large and venomous: they are long gone now, but the two species the komodo dragons once feasted on were miniature elephants!)

It took us only two hours to get back to *Pos 5*. By now, it was hot and the sun harsh, and we slumped in the shade for a rest, meters from the ashes of the fire we had huddled around for warmth only a few hours before. I closed my eyes, and the singing of the wind through the *Casuarina* trees reminded me of beaches in northern Australia. But when I opened them again I could see the first of the stinging nettles and knew the battle with them was about to restart. The forest trees grow thickly here, and an understory of large tree ferns, shrubs of hopwood (*Dodonaea* sp) and a number of small flowering bushes I couldn't identify gave it a magical quality that was only slightly spoilt by the nettles. A single tussock of razor–sharp elephant grass over three meters high sat on the edge of the path and, of course, I sliced my hand open as I passed. It was the only tussock of this grass I saw on the mountain, although I did notice a few near Pancasila, and I wondered whether someone had carried seeds up here during a trek.

"Do you like going up or down," Arman asked.

I thought about it. "Going up is easier if you can go slowly, but going down is hard on my feet—they push against the front of my boots."

These were words I had cause to remember, bitterly, over the next ten hours. The descent was relentless. Down, down, and down. I managed the log bridges without falling into the nettles a second time and remembered the nettle flowers I had head–butted on the way up and avoided them well. I stopped often to photograph interesting things—flowers, bracket fungi on a log, a tree fern unfolding a frond, but this didn't help my feet. By the time we had reached *Pos 3,* they were giving me hell. I took my boots off and viewed my mashed toes, one already blackened by the continual pounding. I dreaded the coming eight or nine–hour walk to Pancasila—over fourteen kilometres of declining track, crawling under logs, slipping on clay, and pushing through unwelcoming brambles.

We had our lunch of more rice and instant noodles, packed up the tent and an extra load of other climbers' rubbish, and headed down. I knew I was in trouble when it took a half hour longer to walk to *Pos 2* than it should have. My feet were not happy.

Somewhere between *Pos 2* and *Pos 1* the path beside me collapsed, and my feet disappeared from under me. I threw myself to the ground to avoid slipping down the embankment into the small creek, which rushed past and climbed back up. Arman began to fuss over me, although there was nothing he could do.

Passing under fallen logs became more of a chore—I could no longer just duck and get through on my haunches; I now had to laboriously get on my hands and knees and crawl under like a two year old. Strangely, the leeches that had enjoyed our company so much the day before had disappeared, and none of us picked up any during the descent at all.

By *Pos 1,* we were an hour behind schedule with eight kilometres to go, and there was no option other than to just plod on, step after step. My camera was now forgotten in my pack, and there was no more procrastinating by taking photos. I became too tired to care about the scratching of the raspberry bushes, and soon my arms looked like bloodied road maps with two highways converging on my left elbow and numerous 'B' roads crossing between them. I got slower and slower but eventually, after an age of walking, I limped into Pancasila like an octogenarian completing his first marathon. It was dark, and I was soaking wet and about as exhausted as I'd ever been.

I farewelled Arman and Herman, who had done their job well. They hadn't been particularly knowledgeable about the plants and animals around—but they knew the annoying plants like the *duli* and *pajatan*, edible birds like the megapode birds (Arman came close to catching one and was clearly excited at the opportunity to eat it), and obvious animals like the deer of the highlands and the monkeys that live around the *Pos 1* and 2 level. They are good bushmen nonetheless and can light fires in the rain using plastic rubbish and burn even the most rain–soaked wood by cutting into it.

They both certainly earned their money. Neither seemed tired after the trip at all and looked as though they could do it again the next day. Arman had walked the entire 42 kilo-metres in his thongs, whilst I struggled in my boots. I was reminded of Saiful's unwelcome comment two nights before:

"You are already old!"

Perhaps he was right, I mused.

I somehow managed to get my boots off, and I threw my seed–riddled socks straight into a bin. I then struggled barefoot to the *mandi* behind Saiful's house for a bath. The water was freezing cold, but I washed nonetheless. Dried blood caked the front of my left foot, and my right foot was already swelling in what would become an attack of gout.

Ten young and fit looking students from Bandung had arrived to climb the mountain. Brimming with life, the girls were giggling like primary school kids at a puppet show, and the boys were larking about like delinquents on holiday. Saiful was pleased; even more so because another eighteen students from a university in Bali were due to arrive the next day. His guest house was filling up, and the mountain was about to get crowded. I was glad I had had it to myself.

While I was doing a bit of first aid on my feet, one of the boys wandered over, I guess just to be friendly and to practice his English. He was slim and small, a handsome youth, half my weight, and young. In fact, he was the last sort of person I wanted to see right then. I looked sourly at his lithe frame, flexing with youthful energy, his stupid face beaming with white teeth and optimism. Like my guides, he probably wouldn't even break a sweat on the climb.

"Hey Boss, how is it, the mountain? Go tomorrow, we." he asked.

"Great," I growled, hoping the leeches and *pajatan* would get him. "Easy for you, have you got a good pair of thongs?" My sarcasm was wasted on him, and he rejoined his silly friends.

Pak Saiful brought me some chicken and rice. I ate the chicken but was unable to look at rice for the next week at least. Then, after drinking a litre of water and feeling feverish after 36 hours of exertions of climbing up and down this incredible volcano on 42 kilometres of narrow mountain trails, I went to bed and slept like the dead Tamboran king for eleven hours.

Chapter 15

The Lessons

Tambora has been traditionally glossed over by historians. Few know anything about it or seem interested and Napoleon Bonaparte and the Battle of Waterloo take precedence in school history books. Also, no one for a long time seemed to care. But volcanoes don't care either; they erupt when they are ready. Gunung Sangeang Api, the very next volcano in the chain going east from Tambora erupted only six days after I had been standing on Tambora's summit, creating a cloud fifteen kilometres high that floated south, dropping ash on Sumba and closing Darwin's airport, some 1300 kilometres away, for two days. What would happen if it had been a Tambora sized eruption? Are we ready? What are the lessons we can learn from the past?

In 1815—16 there was no comprehensive education. Education for most of the world's population was delivered by the religious institutions they happened to be aligned with at birth and much of the world's population could not read or write. There were literate and knowledgeable people, of course, and the 'experts' of the time who could advise governments and business about what was going on, but in a world without the communications infrastructure that only started later in that century, they were operating blind. Many sciences were still in their infancy. No one knew for years what caused the climate anomalies they were experiencing, and they had no way of finding out and no knowledge base upon which to build reasonable theories. They didn't even know if things would return to normal.

The climate anomaly lasted for three years, and earlier chapters outlined some of the greatest difficulties people faced: three years of droughts or floods, heat or cold, riots and starvation, appalling weather or benign weather when it was a monsoon that was actually needed by the long–suffering farmers. The lack of successful crops in both summer and winter in the food bowls of the world meant prices for food that could be imported from elsewhere skyrocketed, and only the rich could afford to eat them.

If Tambora repeated its massive eruption what would be the result? Today Sumbawa has a population of 1.4 million; Lombok has 3.2 million and Bali 4.3 million. Indonesia in total has about 240 million people with nearly 60 per cent of those living on Java. All these people would be at risk, and we can presume millions of them could die.

Volcanoes are monitored by the Indonesian Directorate of Vulcanology and Geological Hazard Mitigation. At Tambora this means their station in the village of Doro Peti (which also offers a shorter route to the summit for travellers than that via Pancasila, although it is more difficult to reach).

The scientists have mapped out a sixty square kilometre 'dangerous zone' they believe will be directly affected by a future eruption and banned people from living here. There is also a larger "cautious" zone of 158 square kilometres which includes a number of villages.

The mountain had been rumbling for weeks. Some people heeded the government's warning and moved outside of the cautious zone. They were camping in school buildings or staying with relatives. The almighty explosion deafened the villagers, and the eruption burst the earth's skin like a humungous boil. It was night, and the tephra plume was quickly as high as 43 kilometres, flashing with lightning—an awesome spectacle.

The noise carried 1500 kilometres, and people in major cities of the region such as Singapore, Kuala Lumpur, Jakarta, and Surabaya were woken and didn't have to be told that there was trouble on the way. Tourists in Bali started phoning their embassies. They tuned into CNN—but they didn't know anything yet. On the mountain pyroclastic winds roared down the slopes followed by super–heated flows of rock. Everything was wiped away or buried. The dawn didn't come—the ash cloud already darkened the skies, as it did 200 years ago, and within days covered an area the size of Australia. All aircraft were grounded, satellite communication was disrupted, and panic and chaos ruled in the streets. In the pitch black of the ash fall, the survivors struggled to hold themselves together. Panicky youths started looting, violently. Parents wanted to ensure the security of their families and started fighting their neighbours for rice or the few palm hearts they could tear out of their gardens.

Many fishing boats were tossed ashore like play–school toys by numerous tsunamis, and others were now on the sea floor or had floated away from broken moorings. It didn't matter—the seas were dead anyway, and the extensive pumice and log rafts made any ship movements hazardous—when boats got stuck in them their sailors had no choice other than to wait for days in the dark, clearing away the ash building up on their decks, until freed by tidal movements.

Richer families had twenty litre bottles of drinking water called 'gallons' that lasted a day or two, but for the majority, there was no clean water anywhere. The wells were poisoned, the pipes were no longer running, ash and pumice had blocked the reservoir and filled the canals. Dysentery arrived and children started bending double with cramps. Many weakened and died.

The government was confused. They had emergency plans in place, but they were woefully inadequate. The plans hoped for lesser eruptions—people were supposed to be evacuated safely, the handful of deaths, which might occur, would be because people had resisted the plan and their roofs had collapsed on them, or they had lost control of their motorbikes in the ash. The army is mobilised, and the soldiers try to retain law and order. Grain stores are open, and Java and wealthy Bali with their huge populations take the lion's share. Better to look after the people you can reach first. And tourists are a priority too, or the international community would complain loudly. Sumbawans have to hold on—a week or two at the most...

International aid groups start rallying. Money starts pouring in. People in rich countries like Australia and Europe have fundraising drives: schools hold quiz nights; Oxfam collects blankets; the Red Cross has a store of emergency tents people will now live in for years; the UN steps in; UNICEF, Doctors Without Borders, USAID, AUSAid, and SurfAid; everyone is ready to help. For several days there is no contact with the Sumbawans. Then navy ships get through and send back the first reports—people need food, water, shelter, and medicine.

There are bodies lying in the streets and washing up on beaches. The risk of disease is increasing. Hundreds of thousands of people are milling round in shock and wasting away. Others are angry—why has help taken so long to reach them? Satellite communication is finally restored as the cloud thins, but the lack of electricity still hampers communications. Solar panels are coated in ash, and some collapse under the weight.

Food production is now impossible, and probably will be difficult for the next eight or nine years: Sumbawa, Lombok, and Bali will need to be fed by others. And the problems are yet to begin in the rest of the world. The expected monsoon will not arrive in India and China. There will be no rice growing there this year either or next. Famine is looming again, but now there are billions of people at risk. In Europe and North America the summer won't return for three years because the North Atlantic Oscillation is disrupted again. The rich countries have larger food reserves these days, but huge populations will eat into them rapidly. Unemployment will rise—there will be no farm work, no processing industries, and no cotton to mill. Lambs will die frozen in the spring, and hoofed animals will find their feet rotting in the mud where the rain doesn't stop or dying of thirst where it never comes. Food prices will start to rise—a loaf of bread $100? Factories will close. Aid may come from areas more fortunate: last time it was Russian grain which saved the Swiss, hit hardest by the anomaly, but this time? Does Russia have excess anymore?

People return to the old ways—foraging for food in the hedgerows—watch out if you are a hedgehog or a snail. Many atheists seek solace in a church because people turn to religion in hard times, shifting the blame, and putting their faith in the hands of others. Churches, mosques, and temples will be full—the religions have never had it so good.

The lunatic fringe find their voice—"The end of the world is nigh!" and religious sects rise and warn that only true believers will prosper as they gather the weak and frightened, promising salvation. Others close their doors and huddle together in compounds, intending to see the bad times through or die together in the sight of God. Inspirational leaders with half–baked theories and hidden agendas take the stage and lead their people to who–knows–where.

Scientists make TV programs about sulphuric acid and climate change. They know all about it these days. In fact, scientists have been warning of a slower, but in the end, no less destructive climate change that we are causing; they call it 'global warming.' Our endless burning of fossil fuels and total dependence on non–renewable carbon–releasing energy forms has had us crawling inexorably to our own destruction for decades. Perhaps now the politicians will listen and find the political will to do something about it. Out of adversity comes change, new ideas arise, new inventions and cultural norms. Perhaps the future will start to look a little brighter. Our life may become simpler, greener, and with a less destructive effect on the planet. Dreams are free.

What about the rest of the planet's beings? We are not alone. With climate change, it is 'cope, adapt or die.' Animals and plants already on the brink of extinction probably won't have a chance. Hundreds of species may be lost. If villagers eat the last wild panda bear to avoid starvation who could blame them? Little is known about the long–term effect on the world's biomes from the 1815 eruption, but now research can be undertaken, papers written, and our understanding of the planet will grow exponentially. Nobel prizes will be won...

Disasters, like wars, bring innovation and change. The *Years Without Summer* of two hundred years ago produced inventions, literature, art, a new religion, mass migration, and new states, new systems of government and public health, poetry, misery, slavery, the new science of meteorology. Family lines were extinguished, and others were created. Migration leads to a greater mixing of the gene pool, and this can make a species stronger. Tambora was a crossroad—people turned one way where otherwise they would have gone the other. How many of us owe our existence to the changes brought about by this mountain and the choices made by our ancestors?

If Tambora or another mountain produced another eruption with a VEI 7 or 8 would we be ready? It's unlikely. Short–sighted political wheels turn slowly—history shows that old civilisations coast into catastrophe, and out of their ashes, like the mythical Phoenix, rise the next. There are still governments in denial about the current climate emergency we are entering, and preparing for a rare possibility of another *Year Without Summer* event is low on everybody's priority risk.

What are the possible protagonists in the next major volcano story we could be experiencing? There are a number of them: Mount Vesuvius is a likely contender, though it is much more likely to have a VEI 4 or 5 eruption. The destroyer of Pompeii and Herculaneum looms over the modern city of Naples in Italy and its three million inhabitants. It will erupt again, perhaps soon, and it has erupted more than fifty times since the big one in AD 79. But if it produced another VEI 5, with a plume extending only thirty or so kilometres upwards, it will not reach the stratosphere and, anyway, it is too far north to have much of a global effect. Its ash cloud will spread widely across Europe and close every downwind airport for days or weeks, and it would certainly not be a good time to be in Naples or the surrounding provinces. The last time it erupted was 1944. Then, it wiped out a few local villages and destroyed eighty of the United States Air Forces' B–25 bombers based at Terzigno as part of the US war effort.

Vesuvius also erupted in 1906 with a reasonably large bang: Naples was devastated, a hundred people were killed, and the city required a costly rebuild. There were no airports to shut down in those days, but a broader effect of the eruption was that the 1908 summer Olympic Games needed a new venue and stepping up to host its first games was the City of London, beating the other contender of the time, Berlin.

The eruption of Vesuvius in AD 79 was a VEI 5, a hundredth the size of Tambora, but most of its eruptions since then have been smaller, and each one reduces the pressure build–up so it is unlikely ever to go off with a VEI 7. The Italian Government's emergency plan for the next one assumes a VEI 4 and involves the evacuation of six hundred thousand people during the week before the eruption. My guess is that many more of the 3 million population will also try to evacuate—imagine the traffic! A bigger eruption than a VEI 4 would really test the plan. The monitoring and the waiting go on.

In the United States, Washington's Mount Rainier is considered a big risk too. Three million people live close to it, and a hundred thousand actually live in houses built on old mudflows, known as *lahars*, from previous eruptions. Scientists say the mountain would give warning of an eruption, but if a lahar was triggered by an unheralded earthquake people would only have minutes to get out of the way.

The beautiful Mount Fuji in Japan has been dormant for three hundred years. Recent earthquakes suggest it might be reawakening, and the 30 million people in Tokyo might need an emergency plan of their own. Plus there are another hundred active volcanoes in Japan for the Japanese to worry about.

In Mexico, Popocatepetl is the second tallest volcano in North America, and it is literally surrounded by people—Mexico City and Puebla together house 20 million or more. Popocatepetl stirred in 2000, and people are worried that it was just a warning of things to come.

There are others too: in the Cameroons, the Congo, New Zealand, Ecuador, Chile, and Colombia and even more in Indonesia, such as Merapi, (which is one of the most active on earth), and every few weeks one or other of the world's volcanoes seems to be playing up.

All these are mostly 'normal' volcanoes: they have a cone, look like the postcards say they should, are dormant for most of the time, but occasionally blow their tops to create various degrees of catastrophe around them. However, there are a very few other volcanoes that we definitely don't want to see erupt again. These are the *supervolcanoes,* the last of which erupted many thousands of years ago.

Lake Toba, on the Indonesian island of Sumatra, is a peaceful inland lake a hundred kilometres long and thirty wide. In its middle is an island named Samosir where the delightful tourist town of Tuk–Tuk wraps the shores with several dozen hotels. The Christian Batak people who live here welcome tourists enthusiastically, run boat tours and snorkelling trips for them and have fish farms and a range of industries around the edge of the lake. Samosir Island is substantial—when I visited, I hired a motorbike and it took most of the day to circumnavigate the island.

At Toba there is no classic cone or shield volcano, it is in fact a depression. The lake is the crater. Super–volcanoes are so big that when they erupt, the entire fabric of the crust of the earth is blown away. Toba expelled at least twenty–eight hundred cubic kilometres of rock and ash into the air, although some scientists claim this to be an underestimation. Scientists have found rocks made of the ash that came from Toba more than two thousand kilometres away in layers that were thirty–five centimetres thick! The whole of South East Asia was buried to an average depth of fifteen centimetres. Even core samples from Lake Malawi in Africa show ash from Toba.

The sulphuric acid layers that developed in the strato-sphere after Toba's eruption reflected the sun's heat, probably for ten years or more, and the earth's average temperature dropped between six and ten degrees Celsius. The earth's climate was significantly altered, and scientists believe it was responsible for decades of colder weather. The eruption also coincides with a thousand year ice age, which left tell–tale signs in the Greenland Ice–sheet, although researchers are divided over whether or not Toba caused this alone.

The research into how Toba affected humans and other species at the time goes on and is not without controversy. The 'genetic bottleneck theory' suggests that about 70,000 years ago the human population of the entire world dropped to less than 15,000 individuals, perhaps as low as 3000 (The chromosomes of other species, such as the orang–utan, gorillas, tigers, and cheetahs provide genetic evidence that shows they also recovered from a very low population base about 70,000 years ago.).

Obviously, humans weren't wiped out, but the catastro-phe likely had an enormous impact on us as a species. The East African homeland of our ancestors probably didn't change too much; there were no glaciers or ice–ages there, but some researchers believe the population stabilised at around 2000 people for several thousand years during this time, so something may have been happening to limit population growth.

Other people had already left Africa and spread east. Stone tools are found both above and below the tephra deposit from Toba at one site in India, showing humans lived there before the eruption and were still there after it. Possibly they were remnant populations and groups of our species were separated from each other for thousands of years and over time developed genetic adaptations to suit the local environment—skin colour, size and shape, lactose tolerance etc. Thus, what Toba may have promoted in our species was the development of differentiation among people, that is, our races.

The second super–volcano of note hasn't erupted for 640,000 years. Some think it has a roughly 700,000 year cycle and will erupt again one day soon. This is Yellowstone in Wyoming, in the United States. Yellowstone sits on a hotspot in the earth's mantle and the super–volcano is a caldera depression nearly a hundred kilometres across. If it ever blows again, we'll certainly be in trouble. Many will die, the great grain producing plains of the USA will be the first to be buried by ash, and the world will reel for decades with the economic fallout.

Scientists continually monitor Yellowstone. There are numerous and regular earthquakes, usually too small to feel, but only weeks before writing this in 2014, there was an earthquake of 4.8 on the Richter scale right in the centre of the caldera. Does increasing activity herald a new eruption? Nobody knows but perhaps. No one knows what it would look like—we've never seen a super-volcano erupt before—but disaster moviemakers are happy to portray them. Both the Hollywood movie *2012* (starring John Cusack in 2009) and the BBC's *Supervolcano* (starring Michael Riley in 2005) portrays Yellowstone destroying the world as we know it.

A third super–volcano is Lake Taupo, on the north island of New Zealand. Taupo erupted 26,500 years ago, ejecting eleven hundred and seventy cubic kilometres of rocks and ash. It is believed that most of the climatic effects were concentrated in the southern hemisphere because of Taupo's high latitude. New Zealand was uninhabited then by humans, but the north island would have been decimated and taken decades to recover.

Taupo has had smaller violent eruptions since, and traces of it have also been found in Greenland's ice. Interestingly, a small eruption from the Taupo region around 200 AD correlates to a year when the skies were reported to be red in Rome and China.

All these volcanoes are still active, and time will reveal their intentions, but to a large extent, we are at their mercy. Learning about the past will help us prepare for the future, if that is what we wish to do, but no one knows when or where the next catastrophe will occur.

Chapter 16

Travel Guide To Tambora

Sumbawa is already on the traveller's map. Surfers discovered it years ago, and the growing number of resorts and hostels suggest a bright future in tourism. Tambora's bicentenary in 2015 and the bicentenary of the *Year Without Summer* in 2016 will bring increased publicity. More people will want to climb to the top and stand like I did, mouth agape, looking into the crater of the largest explosion in 10,000 years.

This chapter offers a short guide to people who want to get there and see for themselves. It is provided in the knowledge that it is not exhaustive, and intrepid travellers will find other unexpected twists and turns in their journey, but it is an offering that may be of use.

Getting to Tambora is not without its challenges. Visitors usually come with a tour group or hire a car and driver from Bima and drive the three or four hours it takes via Dompu and along the Sanggar Peninsula coast road. Much of the road at the time of writing is in good condition, but there are sections where it is deteriorating, and potholes are growing bigger daily. Two sections of dirt road still exist, but work has begun on sealing them. Self–driving cars or motorbikes is easy, and the route there is straightforward with few other roads to confuse.

Another way is to hire a boat from Sumbawa Besar and journey across Saleh Bay to Calabai, and from there seek a car or a motorbike to transport you up to Pancasila. The road up the hill is recently new and still in good condition.

In Pancasila there are two places to stay. Pak Saiful's guesthouse is on the far side of the football field. He has five rooms containing double bunks. In 2014, he was charging 100,000 Rp per night.

The other place is the Tambora Guesthouse, which takes about 15 minutes walking after passing through Pancasila. It is an old coffee plantation homestead, and many of its guests are groups on organised tours. They advertise they are willing to pick you up for 40,000 Rp from Pancasila in their vehicle if you ring ahead.

Pak Saiful displays the walk times and distances on the wall of his *barugaq* and in the guest book. They come from the *Kelompok Pencinta Alam Tambora* (KPAT, the Nature Lovers Group of Tambora) and I found the times suggested were surprisingly accurate, particularly on the way up, and I assume the distances are accurate also (they were probably measured using a GPS). The climb to the summit is divided into six stages, and the descent follows the same path.

Stage		Time Up	Time Down	Distance
1	Pancasila to Pos I (Post 1)	3 hours	3 hours	7.9 km
2	Pos I—Pos 2	2 hours	1.5 hours	3.5 km
3	Pos 2—Pos 3	2 hours	1.5 hours	3.1 km
4	Pos 3—Pos 4	1 hour	45 minutes	1.2 km
5	Pos 4—Pos 5	1 hour	45 minutes	1.2 km
6	Pos 5—Puncak (summit)	3 hours	2.5 hours	4 km
"Pos" = Post			Total	20.9 km
Source: Kelompok Pencinta Alam Tambora, Pancasila			Return	41.8 km

Stage 1: Pancasila to *Pos 1*

This is a long walk of 7.9 kilometres, and the climbing is gentle seems never ending on the return walk). The track starts by following roads through coffee plantations for forty minutes, plunges into the forest for another ten minutes, and then follows an old forestry road, now overgrown with bracken ferns, fishbone ferns, and raspberry bushes. In the late dry season it may be possible to be driven this stretch all the way to Pos 1 on a trail bike. In the morning dew and after rain, brushing up against the plants makes walkers very wet. Suggestions are to wear a long sleeved shirt to avoid scratches from the raspberry plants and two pairs of socks as protection against the leeches, which are numerous if the track is wet. *Pos 1* is a *barugaq* (shelter) in the forest with a piped spring a few meters away providing clean water. A rest here gives you a chance to check for and remove any leeches and have a meal.

Stage 2: *Pos I—Pos 2*

The track from *Pos I* to *Pos 2* starts climbing in earnest. The path is narrow and overgrown with many roots and fallen timbers and vines. Leeches are everywhere. Some sections of clear hard soil are incredibly slippery so beware. The track rises to *Pos 2* with long inclines. There are many logs to climb over or under. *Pos 2* has another tin–roofed *barugaq*. This one is next to a fast flowing stream. There is a flat place to pitch a tent, but the clearing is small.

Stage 3: *Pos 2—Pos 3*

The trail starts to climb more steeply. The forest here has never been logged, but it was completely destroyed by the 1815 eruption. There are steep, slippery sections both up and down through gullies and many fallen logs to climb over or duck under. *Pos 3* is the usual camping site for two–day treks, and the clearing for tents is large and open. There is a *barugaq* here also. The water source is about 200 meters off to the right on a narrow path. You can see the crater rim from here lit up in the afternoon. After six or seven hours walking up, it's a relief to get here. Most two–day trekkers rise at midnight and leave at one am to climb to the summit to see the sunrise. It is cool here, but not cold.

Stage 4: *Pos 3 — Pos 4*

Leaving by flashlight, you follow the steep path up along narrow ridges. The forest is thick and ferns press in on each side, along with other plants that release sticky seeds on your clothing. Then the track enters a thick area of stinging nettles called *pajatan* (or *jelantik*) which are painful, even with a slight brush against the skin. *Pos 4* is a clearing between among very tall, straight trees. It is surrounded by the *pajatan* nettles. Here at 2.30 am it is cold. There is no *barugaq* or water source.

Stage 5: *Pos 4—Pos 5*

Soon after leaving *Pos 4* there is a log bridge about twenty meters long through the nettles to walk along—beware, it is very slippery, and to slip off means painful stings, even through clothing.

There are numerous tree ferns beside the path, and numerous flowering plants and bracket fungi that are worth pausing to look at (on the way down when the sun is up).

The track rises steeply and breathing becomes more difficult with increasing altitude, so numerous short rest breaks are necessary. At this altitude there are no leeches.

Pos 5 is a clearing among *Casuarina* trees and grasses. It is cold here at night but a good place to camp if you have the gear. The guides will suggest you rest here until the right time to make an assault on the summit and arrive at sunrise.

Stage 6: *Pos 5—Puncak* (Summit)

The track rises above the tree line steeply. The forest turns into grasslands as the *Casuarina* trees peter out. Eventually the grasses stop also and are replaced by sparse alpine vegetation like edelweiss. Look out for *kijang* (deer), who live at this altitude. The track flattens out and becomes a weathered rock–scape looking like it belongs on another planet. The crater rim is a plateau several hundred meters broad, and the summit is to the right, easy to spot and an easy climb. The views of the crater are incredible. It is seven kilometres in diameter, twenty–one kilometres in circumference, and 700 or 800 meters deep. It is still active, and clouds of gas blow up in the wind. You can see a green lake on the bottom if the air is clear. Looking west, Mt. Rinjani in Lombok and Mt. Agung in Bali rise above the haze. Look down to view Moyo and Satonda Islands. Look east and you may see Sangeang Api, a small volcanic island north of Bima, which erupted at the end of May 2014.

DESCENDING

The way down is long and tiring, if you are going all the way back to Pancasila it means a 12 hour descent. Going down is where good boots are most needed as you need to avoid the continuing pounding on your toes.

The daylight allows you to look at the views and vegetation you passed when it was too dark to see. Listen out for birds: the *Casuarina* forest has many different types that call to each other regularly, and you can see them because the forest is open (in the lower, thicker forest it is very hard to see any birds, but you will hear them). There are wild pigs (look for the damage they do to the ground) in the forest, and deer in the higher regions. There are macaque monkeys that live around the *Pos 1* and *Pos 2* level.

Watch out for a vicious palm, locally called *duli*, whose fronds work like a climbing vine. It has thousands of sharp hooks which will dig easily into your clothing and skin.

SAFETY:

Pak Saiful's "Guest Book" requires you to record a phone number when you register to climb. Make sure it is a number a rescue party can ring to get help for you, rather than a phone that you carry uselessly in your pack. Ask yourself whom you would like the authorities to contact, if you are in trouble, and provide that number.

Carry a credit card or insurance documents—hospitals will want to see these *before* providing any service (this is good advice for anywhere in Indonesia).

Wear long sleeved clothing against the scratching of the raspberry bushes and ferns.

Stick to the paths—it would be very easy to get lost in the thick forest. Keep away from the edge of the crater—it gives way regularly. You will hear rocks falling. If you are alone, two guides are recommended in case something goes wrong.

CONTACTS and COSTS[1]:

Pak Saiful: Phone (+62) (0) 859 3703 0848, or (0) 823 4069 9138. Pak Saiful operates a guesthouse for 100,000 Rp per bed, and can provide meals at 25,000 Rp each. Pak Saiful does not yet have internet access.

Tambora Guesthouse: Phone +62 (0) 613 5337 0951 visittambora@gmail.com, www.visittambora.wordpress.com : 75,000 Rp per bed and 40,000 Rp for meals. Transport from Pancasila 40,000 Rp.

Guides and Porters charge 150,000—200,000 Rp per person, per day depending on their experience. They will carry the food, water, and camping equipment you need. A few have basic English. Pak Saiful may have some tents available for rent. Small shops in Pancasila sell simple foodstuffs like noodles and rice and local fruit and coffee, anything else you need you should bring. Calabai has more shopping opportunities as it is a larger town.

There was no phone access during my visit to Pancasila or Tambora, though Pak Saiful says sometimes there is using the XL network. (I did successfully use my phone by going about three kilometres down the hill towards Calabai).

There is currently no 'park fee' or permit system to climb the mountain like there is in Lombok for Rinjani, so there are no hidden costs.

---

1   2014 prices — they are subject to change

Further Reading

Websites
Gunungbagging: www.gunungbagging .com
www.visittambora.wordpress.com
www.derekpugh.com.au

Books
de Boer, J.Z. and Sanders, D.T. (2002): *Volcanoes in Human History: the far reaching effects of major eruptions,* Princeton University Press

Klingaman W. and Klingaman N (2013): *The Year Without Summer: 1816 and the Volcano that Darkened the World and Changed History,* St Martins Press

Oppenheimer, C. (2011): *Eruptions that Shook the World,* Cambridge University Press

Raffles, Sir Stamford (1817): *A History of Java*, Cambridge Library Collection 2010

Wood, Gillen Darcy (2014): *Tambora: the Eruption That Changed the World,* Princeton University Press

Wallace, Alfred Russel (1869): *The Malay Archipelago,* John Beaufoy Publishing 2011

Also by Derek Pugh

Turn Left at the Devil Tree

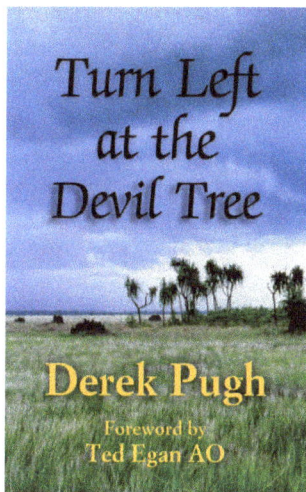

"From the moment he takes the momentous decision to accept a teaching posting at Maningrida, in remote Central Arnhem Land, Australia, Derek develops the best possible tactics in such situations: don't throw your weight around too much; learn from the locals; don't have too big an opinion of yourself; be a good listener:

and... always look on the bright side of life." Ted Egan AO

This delightful book is a slice of history in one of the most remote communities in the world. Full of the people of the bush, the wildlife and extraordinary experiences among a culture witnessed by only a few outsiders, Derek Pugh presents a rare insight into a vanishing world.

Port Campbell Press 2013.
www.derekpugh.com.au
ISBN 9780992355807 Memoir/Australiana

Acknowledgements

My thanks go to my travelling companions Poax Iben and Hughen McConaghy, and to the incredible and hospitable people of Sumbawa—with luck, Tambora will now leave them in peace.

About the Author

Derek Pugh began travelling three days after finishing high school in 1977, but still has plenty in his bucket-list yet to see. He has spent more than a decade travelling and living among Indonesia's volcanoes.

When not on the road he divides his time teaching, writing and raising two lively sons to view the world with awe, respect and wonder. Derek and his family currently live in Darwin, Australia.

Tambora; Travels to Sumbawa and the Mountain that changed the world is his fourth book.

He can be contacted at:
derekpugh1@gmail.com
or via www.derekpugh.com.au.